Digital Marketplaces for Knowledge Intensive Assets

Monetizing and Sharing at Scale

Ranjan Sinha

Cheranellore Vasudevan

MC Press Online, LLC
Boise, ID 83703 USA

Digital Marketplaces for Knowledge Intensive Assets
Ranjan Sinha and Cheranellore Vasudevan

First Edition
First Printing – November 2023

MC Press Online, LLC
Corporate Offices: 3695 W. Quail Heights Court, Boise, ID 83703-3861 USA
Sales and Customer Service: (208) 629-7275 ext. 500
service@mcpressonline.com
Permissions and Bulk/Special Orders: mcbooks@mcpressonline.com
www.mcpressonline.com • www.mc-store.com

ISBN: 978-1-58347-896-7

CONTENTS

ACKNOWLEDGMENTS

We are experiencing a time of seminal transformaton which will influence society in fundamental ways, We are fascinated by the fast emerging field of digital commerce, especially for data, models, and many other digitized assets. This led to the investigative studies around marketplaces for data and AI models which further fueled our interest in narrating the opportunities and challenges and the trends in commercializing the broad set of Knowledge Intensive Assets (KIAs).

It is also a painful realization that book writing is not easy. The strong feeling that we have something important to share kept us going between the stumbling blocks, the "joy of writing," and the professional commitments that make this publication worthy to us. We will be well rewarded if at least some of the readers find the contents meaningful and useful.

We would be deviating from our duty if we didn't mention many professionals and associates who helped us on the journey of publishing this book.

We start with Dr. Inderpal Bhandari, Global Chief Data Officer, IBM, who has always encouraged innovative initiatives in the advanced areas of data and AI and supported us in publishing this work. We gratefully acknowledge Dr. Bhandari for sponsoring the Academy of Technology study on Open Data Marketplaces and encouraging our work on the Marketplace@IBM Council.

Dr. John Cohn, Emeritus IBM Fellow, has always been a source of inspiration in our professional careers at IBM. Many interesting discussions with Dr. Cohn have helped us solidify new ideas and understand the challenges of marketplace and IoT platforms.

We are also indebted to Tom Bellwood, Distinguished Engineer and CTO, IP Legal, IBM, who not only volunteered to be the first "official reader" of our manuscript, but also reviewed the whole book for any IBM intellectual property (IP) infringements.

Besides being an IP expert, Tom Bellwood is also a subject matter expert (SME) on data monetization and marketplaces.

One of the early advocates of our work on marketplaces is Julie Schuneman, Distinguished Engineer and President of IBM Academy of Technology, who understood the significance of the marketplaces business and encouraged our work.

The contributions of Professor Mamnoon Jamil, who served as co-lead of the Data Marketplace Initiative, are valuable and greatly remembered.

The visionary client engagements pioneered by our esteemed IBM colleagues Raquel Katigbak and Mark Thirman have undoubtedly provided valuable insights that we have expressed in this book. A big "thank you" goes to both of them.

We gratefully acknowledge the valuable professional help of Roger E. Sanders and Malati Vasudevan in preparing some of the illustrations and pictures in this book.

Finally, we thank our family members, Chandni Sen Sinha, Lakshmi Vasudevan, and Malati Vasudevan, for their encouragement, support, and patience through this arduous but rewarding journey.

PREFACE

Marketplaces have a unique role in matching supply and demand, creating value for goods—both physical and virtual. Digitization capabilities opened a vast opportunity to record, store, transmit, and trade cognitive assets such as data, models, ads, images, and media products. We call such assets Knowledge Intensive Assets (or KIAs). The novel feature of such assets is that they either are products of creativity or help produce other creative assets. The digital formats of KIAs make them more accessible and valuable commodities that can be traded, often surpassing the value of precious metals, oil, or minerals.

Traditionally, knowledge-based products are offered as a service—e.g., news, books, educational material, and photography. However, the ability to digitally deliver these products led to an explosion of KIA products. The potential market size for KIA products dwarfs any other product suites being commercialized today. At the same time, the monetization of KIA products is accompanied by legal, ethical, and security-centric issues and concerns.

The objective of this book is to compile, analyze, and describe the potential opportunities and associated challenges in the trade of KIA products on digital marketplaces. We have attempted to draw parallels with traditional marketplaces and explain how the functions and capabilities are different in digital marketplaces, especially those that deal with KIA products.

The motivation of writing this book evolved from a series of investigative studies that we conducted on topics such as open marketplaces for data, monetization of Internet of Things (IoT) data, and AI marketplaces under the auspices of the IBM Academy of Technology (AoT). We came across a broad set of emerging platforms that offered trading of various types of KIA products. We also observed the challenges in scaling such platforms and making them commercially successful ventures. We had the opportunity to talk to many stakeholders and subject matter experts (SMEs) who are working in this area. Moreover, we also have our past professional experience in driving the technologies in different marketplace functions, such as optimal selling, personalizing, making recommendations, searching, marketing, and pricing. We noticed that a comprehensive story of digital marketplaces for monetization and the exchange of knowledge intensive entities is not well documented in a book form. We hope this book fills that gap.

We target this book at readers from many professional walks, such as business students and faculty who study and research the science of commerce, producers and owners who want to monetize their KIAs, enterprise companies that want to do business in this field, economists and financial professionals who watch the new patterns of commerce, and the innovative entrepreneurs who bring new ideas to market.

The book has 10 chapters. Among these, we allocated more space to chapters 4 and 5. Chapter 4 focuses on describing the different types of KIAs, their significance, and some emerging players who are already monetizing the KIA products on their digital platforms. The functions and capabilities needed for any digital marketplace are described in chapter 5. A large set of products to trade from a diverse set of producers and a loyal and demanding group of buyers are the key elements of any marketplace. Success and profitability are strongly linked to the volume and ease of transactions happening on the marketplace platforms. Chapter 6 is dedicated to the scaling and automation aspects of digital marketplaces. We have tried to bring in contemporary examples from the industry; however, the field is so turbulent that keeping up with the current state is challenging. We have also attempted to paint what the future may look like and what the burning issues are that need to be addressed by both business processes and technological advancements.

We acknowledge that the topics in some of the chapters need further elaboration—some of them may be worth a book in themselves. We have tried to balance coverage and details and regret any shortcomings. As Keats wrote, "Heard melodies are sweet, but those unheard are sweeter." We leave some of those additional aspects to be penned at a later time.

CHAPTER 1

INTRODUCTION

"Imagination is more important than knowledge. For knowledge is limited, whereas imagination embraces the entire world, stimulating progress, giving birth to evolution."
—Albert Einstein

Inventions, creative products, new processes, and models all emerge from imagination—the ability to think beyond the obvious, to see the unknown, and to embrace risks rather than do nothing.

Marketplaces for virtual assets and finding monetary values for hitherto undervalued knowledge are nothing but results of the imagination of the wise. It's better to visualize and be optimistic about the opportunities to exploit them even if there may be a possibility of proving them to be unrealistic ideas. The motivation to write about Knowledge Intensive Assets (KIAs) and their monetization is inspired by our passion for technology and the great potential we see in the way it influences everyone's lives and businesses.

Knowledge Intensive Assets (KIAs)

KIAs refers to a wide range of virtual assets, such as data, models, digital twins, software, apps, APIs, advertisement templates, courseware, photographs, media products, and similar entities. These sets of assets are named KIAs because either they emerge from domain knowledge or information, or they are used to create new knowledge products. It requires either creative or domain-specific skills to generate and manage such entities. As computing and communication technologies became mainstream in today's world, the type, size, and value of such assets have increased many times.

The power and value of KIAs have become significant. Minerals, metals, and oil were the indicators of wealth in the industrial age. They are being gradually displaced by the volume and value of KIAs. KIA commodities have a combined value much higher than oil, gas, and precious metals like gold and silver. The ownership, exchange, sharing, and monetization of KIA products have assumed a new prominence in today's world. The KIA products exist mostly in digital format. Their exchange and trading are also naturally on digital marketplaces. KIAs have their own peculiar means of storage, transportation, and transfer of ownership.

Marketplaces that trade and monetize KIA products have sprung up all over the world since 2020. These include data marketplaces, AI model repositories, online exchanges for APIs and software, as well as marketplaces for photos, digital twins, cartoons, and courseware. In addition, many services have emerged on digital platforms that more effectively connect the providers and consumers. All of these are contributing factors to the emergence of KIA marketplaces. A detailed discussion on different types of KIA products, their owners, and trading platforms is covered in chapter 4.

What Is a Marketplace?

A marketplace is a forum for sellers and buyers to meet to transact the exchange of goods and services. It can be a permanent location, a physically moving one, or a digital platform. John McMillan in his book *Reinventing the Bazaar*[1], defines market as "a meeting together of people of trade by private purchase and sale" and "a public place where a market is held." He further emphasizes a key characteristic of a market as providing "decision-making autonomy" because the participation is voluntary, and supply and demand dictate the value and transaction decisions.

The difference between a modern digital marketplace and an e-commerce portal is that in a marketplace there is more than one supplier or source of products. In other words, often the goods and services are provided by multiple third parties. It's noteworthy to make the distinction between a hub or showroom (where items are displayed but no transaction may happen) and a true marketplace (where trading—buying and selling—is nearly always happening). Marketplaces can be of two types: specialty markets, such as those dealing only with such goods as auto parts or

1   Reinventing the Bazaar | John McMillan | W. W. Norton & Company (wwnorton.com)

collectibles, or vertical markets that deal in a diversified set of products and services (for example, Amazon, Alibaba, eBay, and TaskRabbit).

Marketplace Economy

The worldwide digital commerce market was estimated to be worth around $5 trillion in 2022 and is expected to grow to $6 trillion by 2024[2]. The top online marketplaces in the world sold $3.23 trillion in goods in 2021. Sales via platforms like those operated by Alibaba, Amazon, eBay, and others accounted for two-thirds of global e-commerce sales in 2022, according to Digital Commerce 360's analysis[3]. The pandemic accelerated the growth of online sales, short-circuiting the previously projected growth of three to five years. It's noteworthy that not just the volume of business increased but the modes of operation also transformed with the help of technology, especially mobile communications.

Many traditional businesses—including hospitals and medical clinics—went digital during this period because of pandemic-forced circumstances. The noteworthy point has been the emergence of the services sector as a major commodity offered on digital marketplaces. The Compound Average Growth Rate (CAGR) of online marketplaces has run to double digits across the global economy, affecting goods and services of all kinds. Global spread of online marketplaces has provided unprecedented opportunities for both sellers and buyers to transact business across continents while continuing to use local currency and local delivery services. While these growth rates have mostly been for traditional physical goods and associated services, the market for KIA products is still to be fully accounted for and is growing fast. The Accenture Report[4] projects the market value only for data, and its derivatives alone could hit more than $4 trillion by 2030, surpassing any other single traded commodity. Combining the markets for courseware, ads, generative AI, and software, the value of transactions of KIA products through online marketplaces can be astounding.

About This Book

This book is intended to give readers a good perspective of the promises and challenges of online marketplaces for "virtual products." In the near future, these are going to provide more worth via both monetization and usage than traditionally traded physical

2   https://www.insiderintelligence.com/insights/ecommerce-industry-statistics/
3   https://www.digitalcommerce360.com/article/infographic-top-online-marketplaces/
4   https://www.accenture.com/us-en/insights/high-tech/dawn-of-data-marketplace

commodities. The list of KIAs is growing, triggered by advances in technology and the discovery of novel use cases and applications.

To begin, the book narrates the history of trading and explains how technology fueled the launch of online marketplaces. Chapter 3 covers a representative set of marketplace players and chronicles the means by which they became dominant, their particular roles, their influence, and their economic impact. The KIAs are described in detail in chapter 4, which also covers their characteristics, the relevance of each of them, and the ways they are exchanged and monetized today. The functions that are essential for marketplace operations, along with tools and technologies currently supporting them, are explained in chapter 5.

The scaling and growth of marketplaces of all types need automation at every step of their operations. Chapter 7 touches on the types of automation and corresponding tooling available. Chapters 8 and 9 are about the social and cultural impacts of digital marketplaces on our society and human behaviors. The pros and cons of online shopping can be interesting to note. In conclusion, the book covers some emerging trends and future pathways for digital marketplaces, especially for KIA products.

CHAPTER 2

THE EMERGENCE OF COMMERCE

"Those who fail to learn from history are doomed to repeat it."
—Winston Churchill

Introduction

Commerce adds value to goods and services. While the cost of producing an artifact or rendering a service has an influence on the value or price, cost is mostly determined by market demand. Imagine the scenario of crude oil being available for free or with a negative price in 2021[5]! That actually happened. The supply-demand nexus has decided the flow of commerce beginning at the time of barter economy (6000 BC) and progressing up to the speculative bids and virtual transactions of today.

---

5   https://www.weforum.org/agenda/2020/04/oil-barrel-prices-economic-supply-demand-coronavirus-covid19-united-states/

Figure 2.1: Trading Post

The term "trading post" originally comes from the western settlement era. Trails between trading posts were known as trade routes. Usually, goods were traded on a barter system, with no need for money.

Commerce is the pulse of any economy and will remain so until the day all people on the planet have either become self-sufficient or no longer have any needs or wants. Obviously, both are practically impossible. In his book *Reinventing the Bazaar*[6], John McMillan mentions this Vietnamese proverb: "Trying to stop a market is like trying to stop a river." The stubbornness of the seller is driven by the demand for goods offered. This tension leads to new ways of identifying buyers and new ways of selling and buying. This chapter briefly outlines the emergence and progression of trade and commerce from their early beginnings to current practices.

The Beginnings of Trade

Historically, the flow of goods and associated trading dictated the emergence of a new socio-economic-political fabric and often resulted in development of civilizations like

6   Reinventing the Bazaar | John McMillan | W. W. Norton & Company (wwnorton.com)

those that profited from the first ever recorded (120 BCE) trade route—the Silk Road. Trade along the Silk Road economic belt included many things beyond silk, such as fruits and vegetables, livestock, grain, leather and hides, artwork, precious stones, metals, and perhaps most importantly, language, culture, religious beliefs, philosophy, and science. For example, the Silk Road is credited for the spread of Buddhism, but also for a notorious disease—the plague—across continents.

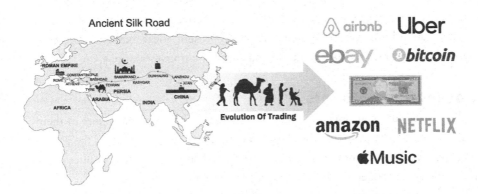

Figure 2.2: Historical Evolution of Marketplaces

Markets have existed ever since people began wanting to monetize or exchange the goods they produce, own, or broker. The earliest bazaars are believed to have originated in Persia as early as 3000 BCE, and from there they spread to the rest of the Middle East and Europe[7]. This perspective is significant even today, 2200 years later. The route has changed from mountain ranges and seaports to digital media networks, even though the objectives and scope of trade and commerce remain the same. However, the manner of trading and the types of goods and services exchanged have been undergoing a major evolution during recent years. This has resulted in innovative patterns of commerce and associated business culture. The faster route of communications and the proliferation of transactions over networks enabled by a cloud infrastructure are helping the marketplace business flourish. At the same time, the same trends have also introduced concerns and new requirements for safety, security, privacy, and trust.

The Modern Marketplaces

The digital marketplaces of today are worth trillions of dollars. Today's successes—which range from small-scale retailer online e-commerce marketplaces to large

7   https://en.wikipedia.org/wiki/Marketplace

enterprises like Amazon, Alibaba, and Walmart—prove that opportunities are still not fully tapped. As these online traders have grown, they have introduced innovative business models, such as those used by Airbnb, Uber, Netflix, and Indeed. The traditional brick-and-mortar companies like Walmart have also jumped into the fray. The Airbnbs, Ubers, iTunes, Netflixes, LendingTrees, and Instacarts not only created different models of selling and buying, but also made some significant changes in many industries in terms of promoting amateur and small-scale players and shifting the way intellectual properties (IPs) are published and monetized. In addition to the significant transformation in the ways of commerce they represent, these example companies also represent milestones of major cultural and economic transformations.

Marketplace Models

Marketplaces can be grouped in multiple dimensions based on the nature of their operations, their types of stakeholders (producers and consumers), and their types and ranges of products. Although a marketplace, in its purest definition, implies commercial transactions, a broader view should consider non-commercial ones too.

Based on intended audience, marketplaces can be classified as "internal," "consortia," or "public."

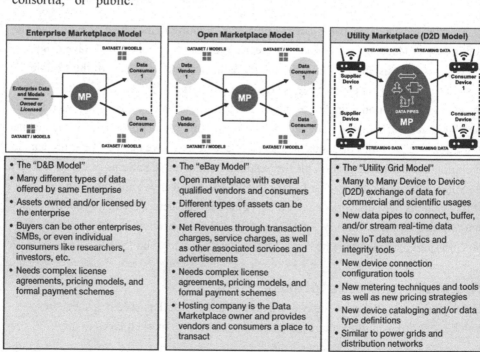

Figure 2.3: Marketplace Models

Internal marketplaces are common in large enterprises, where all assets and products are curated, cataloged, and governed on a single platform for the consumption of their employees. These may include both internally and externally sourced products and services. The main objective of such marketplaces or hubs is to provide a single-stop shop for most commonly needed goods. The internal marketplaces or hubs also promote cost reduction by avoiding duplication, enabling uniformity, and standardizing purchase and consumption by everyone within the enterprise.

Each individual user who consumes assets doesn't directly pay for the goods' value, because a corporate budget allocation covers the procurement and other logistics expenses. Typical examples of such products include computing devices, software licenses, stationery, and airline tickets. The corporate procurement department verifies needs, negotiates prices, finalizes sales contracts with vendors, and catalogs the products, as well as monitors and meters the consumption levels.

Consortia marketplaces are structures in which a cooperating set of organizations come together to share or sell products among the members of the consortium. For instance, suppliers, manufacturers, and sales dealers may form a common marketplace to catalog and share their assets.

Open (aka "public" or third-party) marketplaces are probably the truest representation of a market. They are called "open" because the sets of providers and consumers aren't restricted (other than for broad user validation). The open marketplace doesn't necessarily hold a full set of assets. Alternatively, the marketplace platform may carry a catalog of products and enable the transactions. A well-known example, Alibaba[8], one of the largest retailers, doesn't keep any inventory. Order execution is typically handled by the asset owners or providers.

Another way to group marketplaces is based on the way they are implemented, as illustrated in the figure below. It's important to note the different business models and their stakeholders because the online marketplace arenas also have equivalent replicas of these models.

8   https://www.alibaba.com

Marketplace as an Offering	Marketplace as a Service	Marketplace of Marketplaces
 • Tools • Platform • Functions		
• Self-contained-packaged solution that can be a product offering • Provides a solution that has all components needed to establish and run a marketplace • Clients could launch a marketplace by populating the trading assets and managing the operations • Tools and platform need to genericized for the smooth adoption by different types of industries	• Platform, tools, content development, and operations are all done as a service -turnkey for any enterprise • Establish, replenish, and manage the marketplace for a client • Similar to IT services outsourcing and closer probably, to IBM B2B Commerce approach	• A container of multiple marketplaces where each cover different categories of product assets • A kind of "Super Shopping Mall" for single-stop-shopping with different groups of vendors • Share common functions such as check out, user account management, payments, order management, etc.

Figure 2.4: Digital Marketplace: Types of Offerings

Marketplace as an Offering can be viewed as a prepackaged solution in which users may "buy" the solution and launch a marketplace by populating it with the assets the users want to commercialize. Such a "wrapped" marketplace package includes all necessary functions, like catalogs, search engines, shopping carts, billing and payment schemes, and associated tools to quickly productionize a fully loaded marketplace platform.

Marketplace as a Service is another form of implementation, one in which the marketplace provider hosts the platform and manages the operations on behalf of its clients. The ownership of assets, revenue, and ultimate responsibility lies with the marketplace owner, while the operations and management are supported by a technology-cum-business outsourcing agency. This arrangement enables the marketplace owner to focus on its core business of vendor development, pricing, order execution, and business policies, while the infrastructure and tooling are supplied and operated by a technology company.

A third dimension, *Marketplace of Marketplaces,* is analogous to a super shopping mall that provides a common infrastructure and tooling across multiple shops or marketplaces. The vendors are shop owners who can bring in their assets and trade them with the help of built-in common facilities. Payments, billing, and shipping are commonly managed by the "mall" owners.

Disruptive Marketplaces

Disruptive marketplaces create new types of transactions that draw in buyers and/or sellers who weren't already participating in that market[9], functionally creating new kinds of transactions that weren't possible before. A good example is Uber[10], which offers ride-sharing transactions that weren't previously available. Priceline[11] is an example in which the consumer can specify a price and the suppliers compete to meet or nearly match that price. Airbnb[12] created new sets of suppliers who could share their spare space. Examples of new suppliers are marketplaces such as Substack[13] (an online platform for writers), and Patreon[14] (a membership platform for creatives), which have made it substantially easier for writers, artists, and others to market and monetize their expertise and skills, unlocking a new talent pool. Real-estate listing portals like Zillow[15], Compass[16], and Redfin[17] disrupted the real-estate market, which was previously closely controlled via secret Multiple Listing Service (MLS) listings. Zillow then started making outright purchases directly from sellers, cutting into the business of traditional real-estate agents.

The underlying recipe for disruption is identifying the friction, inefficiency, or blockages in the demand-supply network and removing them by using technology, new business models, and new awareness.

Recap

Digital transformation is accelerating online marketplaces not only by making it easier to buy and sell, but also by connecting societies, opening new revenue streams, and in a way, democratizing commerce by making things available to anyone at any place at any time. The business models may vary and may eventually be transformed based on the types of goods traded, geography, local culture, and economy. However, the impact of these online trading hubs is becoming more significant to all walks of life.

---

9   https://hbr.org/2021/05/what-makes-an-online-marketplace-disruptive

10 www.uber.com

11 https://www.priceline.com

12 https://www.airbnb.com/

13 https://substack.com/

14 https://www.patreon.com/

15 www.zillow.com

16 www.compass.com

17 www.redfin.com

CHAPTER 3

TECHNOLOGY FOR DIGITAL COMMERCE AND PLATFORMS

"The human spirit must prevail over technology."
—Albert Einstein

Introduction

Several technological components support the growth of digital commerce. Some of these are the internet, cloud computing, digital payments, and smart devices, as well as search, advertising, personalization, and language-translation services. In general, connectivity, automation of commerce functions, digital interfaces, and digital media are the backbone of digital marketplaces. This chapter covers a few currently dominant components and some emerging ones. Descriptions and observations about some major digital marketplace players are also included to provide historical and contemporary perspectives of this transformation of online trade.

The Internet

Two major technologies that led to digital platforms, digital commerce, and associated ecosystems are the internet and the cloud.

The internet made it possible to connect remote machines and people across continents. The advances in the speed and bandwidth of these electronic networks enabled communications, sharing, and transactions almost in real time between people who have never met and are unlikely to ever meet. It opened a host of virtual markets for different types of commodities across the globe. For example, flowers from Kenya are auctioned in European-centric marketplaces, but eventually these perishable goods are made available in distant places like Seoul. The high-speed connections enabled by 3G to 6G networks and the remotely connected computing and storage platforms are the core technologies behind digital platforms, even as the massive commercial transactions are fueled by other associated technologies, such as digital payments, mobile devices, personalized interfaces, and secured services for storage, sharing, trading, and currency exchange.

Cloud Computing

"Cloud" is a metaphor for the internet. Often anything remote over the internet is represented with a "puff cloud" depiction. Literally and functionally, cloud computing entails data, storage, and computing happening remotely. Essentially, it's a remote computer data center with hardware and software that serves one or more concurrent users. While technically an extension of the classic client-server model, cloud computing principles offer a set of shared and theoretically unlimited computing and storage resources. End users do not have to worry about buying, owning, or maintaining any infrastructure; instead, they pay per use as demand changes.

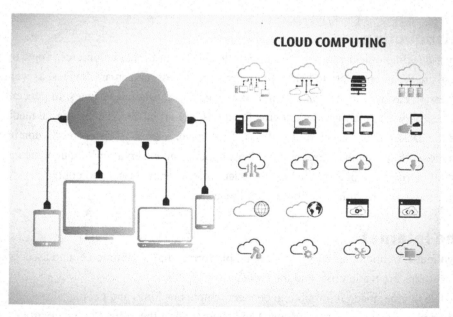

Figure 3.1: Cloud Computing

The advantages of cloud computing are well known and include advantages for users, such as avoiding upfront infrastructure costs, providing better business agility via spinning off new services quickly, meeting the varying demands of IT workloads by appropriately scaling up or down, paying for services based only on consumption, and assuring better reliability and availability. However, this technology introduces concerns of security, privacy, lack of in-house development capability, ambiguity of service-level agreements (SLAs), and the uncertainty of future charges, all of which hinder universal adoption of a public cloud infrastructure.

Public cloud involves cloud services being provided to enterprises exclusively by third-party providers. Private cloud, an infrastructure under which one corporate entity manages its own remote servers and services via the internet, is often a larger responsibility than many enterprises care to assume. The most common version of cloud today is the hybrid cloud, a mixed computing architecture in which the applications and storage can be supported by different environments, which may include partial public-cloud and private-cloud structures, as well as on-premises data centers or "edge" computing locations.

Hybrid cloud computing approaches are widespread because most users rely on different types of clouds and standalone computing platforms, often used in a distributed fashion. Hybrid cloud solutions enable users to migrate and manage workloads between these various cloud environments, helping enterprises dynamically adjust their computing resources to meet specific business needs. Many organizations choose to adopt hybrid cloud platforms to reduce costs, minimize risk, and extend their existing capabilities to support digital transformation efforts.

Digital Payments

If there is a single most important function that proliferated e-commerce and online marketplaces, it's digital payment methods. The online payment process started with prepaid credits and progressed through bank debit cards, plastic credit cards, departmental credit cards, and gift cards. Those processes have now progressed to electronic bank transfers, electronic bill payments, e-checks, and wire transfers, as well as modern mobile digital payment schemes such as PayPal, Venmo, and Zelle. In addition, there are now digital wallets such as Apple Pay, Google Pay, and Samsung Pay; virtual credit cards issued by banks for contactless payments using near-field communication (NFC) technology and magnetic secure transmission (MST) technology; and cryptocurrencies like Bitcoin and Ethereum.

Besides enabling online transactions, the digital payment methods have proven to be more convenient, easier to use, fully secure, and flexible for small and large payments across the globe[18]. Digital payments must solve multiple issues, although most of them are already well addressed. These include currency conversion and tax computation based on place of sale and location of customer. Some equally important challenges are to offer secure financial transactions and protect consumer privacy. Digital payments also entail technical solutions for digital billing and related communications.

Digital payments[19] are applicable not only to buyers, but also to vendors. The royalty and incentive payments to vendors and any outright purchases need to be properly accounted for and tallied, and payments must be automatically generated to scale up marketplace operations.

Several payment-processing technologies exist today, along with the appropriate security controls. Some of the payment functions are further detailed in chapter 5.

Metaverse

If internet and electronic payments have accelerated the growth of e-commerce, metaverse-related technologies are expected to take online or virtual shopping to the next level by providing a more immersive experience for selecting and evaluating products, as well as handling sale and resale functions. One good example is Decentraland[20].

If anyone has missed the chaos, shouting, sweat, anxiety, and excitement of Wall Street stock exchange floor trading, metaverse can possibly simulate the same environment with expert "avatar traders," which refers to a whole new world of regulation, certification, legal clearance, liability, and record-keeping challenges.

Metaverse can have four major impacts for marketplaces:

- 3D product catalogs for more immersive search experiences
- New ways of testing and experimentation with goods before the user makes the final decision to purchase (similar to today's test driving of a new car before a user purchases it)
- New categories of digital artifacts as non-fungible tokens (NFTs) (digital replicas of physical goods)
- New self-directed avatars that will do the bidding, selling, bargaining, making of payments, and executing of orders

18 https://www.entrust.com/resources/faq/guide-to-digital-payments
19 https://www.mckinsey.com/industries/financial-services/our-insights/banking-matters/new-trends-in-us-consumer-digital-payments
20 https://market.decentraland.org

Most of these visionary concepts may appear to be science fiction today. It isn't clear how and when these will become commercially available, but they will need to include built-in safety, security, and privacy features.

The Horizon platform developed by Meta (formerly Facebook) and the HoloLens platform of Microsoft are groundbreaking developments in building interactive communities for collaboration, communication, sharing, and handling of commercial as well as personal interactions and transactions. NVIDIA's Omniverse is another great example. Apple's platform as well needs to be mentioned. Such services help businesses bring together various digital assets, irrespective of their formats or engines, into a single virtual environment.

On his website[21], venture capitalist Matthew Ball describes metaverse as "a massively scaled and interoperable network of real-time rendered 3D virtual worlds. These virtual worlds can be experienced synchronously and persistently by an effectively unlimited number of users with an individual sense of presence, and with continuity of data, such as identity, history, entitlements, objects, communications, and payments[22]."

Metaverse was first described by sci-fi author Neal Stephenson in his novel *Snow Crash*. It could become a reality as several large technology companies are investing in supporting technologies. Facebook CEO Mark Zuckerberg rebranded Facebook as Meta[23] and announced its virtual work environment. NVIDIA is promoting its Omniverse to enterprises, introducing its graphic engines and technologies[24] to create 3D assets. Microsoft recently announced the acquisition of Activision[25] in the gaming area. These are efforts mainly focused on the general entertainment industry, although offshoots will be spreading to other commercial applications.

Given the current pace of activity, it appears that in less than a decade, commercial portals (which are mostly 2D web portals today) will be based on metaverse technology. This means small, medium, and large enterprises will have their products cataloged, their information shared, and their interactions facilitated via "metaverse world platforms." This will entail several enhancements—or rather a metamorphosis— of the current 2D web portals, particularly in terms of information display, product

21   https://www.matthewball.vc/all/themetaverse
22   https://www.matthewball.vc/the-metaverse-primer
23   https://about.fb.com/news/2021/10/facebook-company-is-now-meta/)
24   https://www.nvidia.com/en-us/omniverse/
25   https://news.microsoft.com/2022/01/18/microsoft-to-acquire-activision-blizzard-to-bring-the-joy-and-community-of-gaming-to-everyone-across-every-device/

cataloging, the processes of buying and selling, customer support, and other related functions. Other components that will play well into this new mix are digitized assets such as digital twins. The interfaces, interactions, and business values derived in the coming decade could be illuminating.

Current Major Marketplace Players

There are thousands of digital commerce players today, led by giants like Google, Amazon, Alibaba, and eBay. Presenting a comprehensive list of all current marketplace players here isn't feasible and will be rendered obsolete in no time. This section discusses some of the major players that are significant in terms of their volume of business, the technology behind them, and the economic or market influence they have. These were chosen based on specific considerations. eBay is possibly the first large-scale commercially successful marketplace platform. Amazon, of course, is the largest marketplace, with its own dynamics and reach today. Priceline shot into fame because of its pricing model of the commodities with which it deals (airline tickets primarily). Uber not only changed the whole personal transportation model, but also demonstrated how a "crowd-sourced supplier network" can be quickly and successfully built within a massive network of service providers and consumers.

eBay

eBay[26] is an early example of a successful commercial marketplace. It started in San Jose, California, in 1995. It uses a simple yet highly effective business model: bringing buyers and sellers together in one online platform and charging a fee for any transactions completed. This has been emulated since by many other marketplaces, including Amazon.

eBay started its business by listing a printer for $1 and has now grown to become a more than $30 billion market-cap company. It's currently a global e-commerce powerhouse with more than 200 million registered users and a highly successful mobile app that's been downloaded more than 500 million times, according to company data. More than 19 million sellers have listed approximately 1.6 billion products on this marketplace.

While bidding in auctions is free to buyers, the seller is charged an immediate insertion fee and an additional fee for special promotions, such as marking products using bold fonts that enable a particular item to stand out from competitors. Moreover, a final fee is attached at the close of a transaction, which ranges between 1.25 and 5

26 www.ebay.com

percent of the final sale price, depending on the item sold on the platform. eBay earns its fees by listing the item and notifying sellers when their auction-price level was met or exceeded. The buyer and seller handle most of the details of the transactions, including closing the deal independent of eBay. This is a true enabler or brokerage model mimicking typical physical marketplaces that give space for transacting business.

Amazon

Amazon[27] is the "800-pound gorilla" in the world of marketplaces. Amazon is also a good example of how a business can push technology trends, such as employing cloud, enhancing the user experience, deploying robotics, and showing how scaling can be accelerated with automation. The details of Amazon's business and products should be well known to most readers. At the same time, it's helpful to record some observations and practical lessons that may be useful for anyone in the marketplace business.

One of the greatest—and perhaps most obvious—lessons Amazon illustrates is that if there is a single factor that's the greatest cause for any marketplace's success, it's scaling, particularly in terms of product range and diversity of suppliers. "Growth facilitates growth" essentially means that more products and suppliers attract more consumers and buyers, who in turn bring in additional suppliers. Amazon has shown that this self-propelled growth is possible only when a marketplace reaches a critical threshold of scale. The rate of scaling up is fueled by many factors but can be mainly attributed to technology-driven automation in all aspects of supply chain and commerce, as well as the ease of doing business transactions. (Automation in the marketplace is covered in a later chapter.)

There are several lessons of success and failure that observers can learn from the world's largest retailer. Some of those can be summarized as follows.

Profits take time. One of the lessons Amazon taught marketplace enthusiasts is about its resilience against vicissitudes of market reactions. Making profits in marketplaces, especially in retail, requires wisdom-driven patience and a critical level of business maturity in terms of the number of vendors, goods, and consumers.

User experience is the key. The "Amazon experience" has become synonymous with providing an exemplary user experience. The "one-click purchase" is not just a cliché but a well-thought-out design based on user behavior analysis. It's not surprising that the patented technology[28] that can anticipate orders and deliver them to the doorstep

---

27 www.amazon.com

28 https://worldwide.espacenet.com/publicationDetails/biblio?CC=US&NR=5960411&KC=&F T=E&locale=en_EP

is not just an attempt to delight the customer, but a key ingredient in the process of filling the cash register as well. Several factors contribute to this achievement, such as discovering the right product, providing rich and accurate product information (including reviews and ratings), engineering the ease of completing a purchase, facilitating the speed of delivery, and importantly, offering the confidence of a no-questions-asked and no-penalty return facility. These aspects are carefully crafted and nearly perfected in the Amazon world, which is the open secret of their success.

These are well-tried traits of any retail operation. However, the key to making Amazon massive and scalable in popularity and volume has been the adoption of technology at every step. Focusing on technology to make the transactions and perform associated services is equally important. The business practices of offering Amazon Prime and Amazon credit cards are also important aspects in Amazon's toolbox. The availability of "anything under the sun" and quickness of delivery are possible only because of its invention and adoption of the latest technologies for automation and personalization.

Priceline

Priceline[29] is the first online company that introduced the concept of a "name your price" model for online travel- and tourism-related services. In the traditional business world, this is an age-old practice. When there's an excess of inventory, especially if it's time-bound and perishable, it's best to offer it at a discounted price. However, many times, the supplier or service provider may not know what to ask for fear of losing the business. Enabling the consumer to bid on a price eliminates the uncertainty of transactions if the provider can agree to that price. The model is simple. Without revealing who the supplier or provider is, the platform can offer a deal telling buyers to name a price at which they will make the commitment to buy. This deal can be taken to multiple competing suppliers to match the buy offer. A small fee is charged if the deal goes through.

During the late '90s, when the internet was proliferating and the masses started to make travel reservations online, this model introduced by Priceline that connects consumers to travel service providers—such as airlines, hotels, and rental cars—became an instant success. It's a win-win for both service providers and consumers, optimizing providers' underutilized resource capacity (e.g., seats, space) and giving consumers a discounted price for the same services. Priceline addresses the scenario by quietly selling off supply overhang while giving consumers the satisfying price they are seeking. Priceline has grown to about $15 billion in annual revenue and maintains several subsidiaries like Rentalcars.com and OpenTable.

29   https://www.businessinsider.com/how-pricelines-business-works

Uber

Uber probably pioneered the "crowdsourcing" of suppliers. The "Uber Model," as it's often referred to, is an arrangement in which the supplier and consumer are loosely connected for a service, and the job of the platform is merely making a transient on-demand connection between them. Of course, the success of crowdsourcing is mostly centered around smooth billing, service provider vetting, and overall governance to provide friction-free service execution.

It's worthwhile to note that the success of Uber is in its quick and easy scaling without much infrastructure investment. This is a textbook example of the power of using available technology in new business ways. The success of Uber's transportation business dramatically led to many spinoffs and new ventures in all sorts of businesses, such as TaskRabbit, which provides, for example, handyman labor, dog walking, home delivery of foods, and equipment- and appliance-installation/assembly.

Indeed

Indeed is highlighted here mainly because of the acceleration of its growth with the right business strategy, grounded on the strength of its technology. Online job postings and recruiters like Monster, Hired, job.com, and many other smaller players were in place a long time ago. The recruitment companies and online portals of employers were also competitive places for a job search. However, Indeed rightly invested resources to become the "Google for jobs" by offering connectivity, compilation, and networking of employers, recruiters, and job seekers. A mix of strong entrepreneurship and a technology vision fueled Indeed's rapid rise to become the strongest player in the marketplace for jobs, with more than 300 million unique visitors every month. It not only facilitates job searches, but also enables posting of resumes and researching of companies by job seekers. For the employers, Indeed provides several (paid) services to short-list candidates, such as conducting interviews and advising on compensation. These services are greatly beneficial for small business owners who may not have a functional HR department for employee recruitment. It's amazing to note that Indeed is a powerhouse, with 12,000+ employees and worldwide business operations.

Meta

No marketplace article or book would be complete without mentioning Meta (formerly known as Facebook), which has revolutionized the way people connect and communicate and is likely the best example (next only to mobile phones) of how to embed technology deeply into the daily lives of ordinary people. Meta tapped right into people's quest to share and communicate remotely. Meta enables users to inform their circle of friends about all the good and bad things happening in their lives—the events, milestones, and emotions—easily and widely. Also important are the multi-modal ways—photos, videos, and audios—Meta users can employ to transcend the limitations of language, distance, and even the traditional social boundaries of privacy. What Meta has facilitated is empowering even those people who are often shy or incapable of effective communication to share information.

Connecting people is indeed a significant phenomenon, and Meta did it with the help of technology. The openness of this connectivity, of course, has raised concerns about issues of privacy, security, and even addiction to the tool. Setting aside the potential dangers of spreading false information and potential criminal activities indirectly facilitated by such platforms, Meta has paved the way to a new, powerful, and easy-to-use platform for communication and sharing.

While the social impact is well known, one cannot underrate the technology enablement. The personalization of interactions, machine learning (ML)-enabled reporting, promotion, self-propelled network recommendation, and interest-centric pushes of notifications are excellent examples of how business scenarios can flourish with the use of new technologies. Meta is now equally famous as a technology house—for obvious reasons—as it needs to retain and grow its billions of consumer users. Its contributions to AI, data science, search, cloud, and digital media technologies are commendable.

Netflix

Netflix is the "poster boy" for digital marketplaces. Business schools teach its model and portray it as the "killer of the brick-and-mortar video business." Netflix can be characterized as having been the right venture at the right time for the right commodity. The audio and video turned digital with the introduction of the widely accepted MP3 and MP4 formats. The home internet connectivity speeds increased manyfold and became cheaper. The result was the opportunity to easily deliver movies and songs in downloadable or streaming modes. The resulting demise of old media shops like Blockbuster is a popular story of internet marketplace success.

The ease of searching and accessing entertainment products from one's own home not only disrupted the consumption of entertainment products, but also made some strong impacts on the production and release of the media products. With the attempt and subsequent success in moving beyond the marketplace for digital entertainment products, Netflix emerged as first a release platform and then as a production platform, an evolution that shows its business acumen. However, traditional production companies like Walt Disney immediately followed the same path. Also jumping into the fray have been communication companies like AT&T and technology companies like Apple and Amazon, all of which have started streaming, media production, and release operations themselves, trying to beat Netflix at its own game. However, Netflix lays claim to being the forerunner of the digital media marketplace.

iTunes

iTunes is mentioned here because it's a prime example of how a platform and an associated device can enable a new way of commodity trading and how the company and the technology mutually benefit. Importantly, there's no existence of one without the other. When Apple announced smartphones (iPhones)—with a built-in media player, internet connection, and camera— it was the beginning of a clever integration of seemingly disparate technology plays. Steve Jobs' vision led to the hitherto unheard of practice of integrating multiple functions into a single device, which made it a real personal digital assistant (PDA). One of the smart business strategies was to start the "media shop" as an app and support the shop with a multitude of common consumer vendors. Perhaps Uber learned from the iTunes business model. Who would have thought $1 to $5 assets that are sold through a tiny device could eventually grow to a $20 billion business for Apple? Its success is due to facilitating the ease of purchasing, downloading, and maintaining multiple media assets on the same device. (In fact, this was supplemented by Apple Pay later.) The smooth and seamless integration of all steps of cataloging, searching, promoting, purchasing, downloading, and playing (using) being available on the same device is an engineering marvel and a smart business move by Apple.

Alibaba

Alibaba[30] was originally established to be the e-commerce model for small and medium Chinese companies to sell their goods worldwide. It grew to become the sixth largest global commercial enterprise and has become a holding company of several e-commerce marketplaces. Alibaba's core business resembles that of eBay, in which it acts as an agent between buyers and sellers and facilitates the sale of goods between the two parties via its extensive network of websites.

Alibaba's largest site, Taobao, is a marketplace in which neither sellers nor buyers are charged a fee for completing transactions, but sellers pay to rank higher (for

30 https://businessmodelanalyst.com/alibaba-business-model/

advertising) on the site's search engine, generating advertising revenue for Alibaba. This model contrasts with the largest e-commerce retailer (Amazon), which directly sells goods it sources from manufacturers while retaining only a small percentage of third-party product inventory.

Alibaba's TMall[31] is an e-commerce outlet that caters to well-known brands such as Gap, Nike, and Apple. Alibaba generates revenue not only from transactions, but also through annual user fees and advertisements. It has ventured into the financial space through its Alipay digital payment applications. Alibaba invests on the technology front as well through cloud, data, and AI business applications.

TaskRabbit

TaskRabbit[32] is an online and mobile marketplace that matches freelance labor with local demand, enabling consumers to find help with everyday tasks such as moving, cleaning, running errands, decorating, assembling furniture, and yard work. It operates an "odd-job service" in more than 60 U.S. cities and connects users, called taskers, to paying gigs. Taskers set their own rates and may get tips. Founded in 2008 as RunMyErrand, TaskRabbit currently has tens of thousands of taskers available to help consumers across a wide variety of categories. The volume of tasks, such as 2.5 million furniture assembly tasks and 1.2 million moves, shows the heavy demand for one-time contract jobs needed in many households. TaskRabbit collects as their fee a fixed percentage of payments for tasks completed, which is its major source of income. Its annual revenue is estimated to be more than $250 million.

Recap

It is illuminating to observe the diversity of marketplaces that were never thought of or imagined before their times. These businesses are examples of innovation, entrepreneurship, advances in technology, and the evolution of the socio-economic fabric. These marketplaces not only reflect the new ways of trading, but also drive new economic growth and improve living standards. In many ways, these are indicators of beneficial transformations caused by innovations in technology and business models.

---

31 https://www.alibabacloud.com/customers/tmall
32 https://www.taskrabbit.com/

CHAPTER 4

KNOWLEDGE INTENSIVE ASSETS (KIAs) FOR TRADING

"Knowledge is the only asset that nobody can steal from you."
—Anonymous

Introduction

Marketplaces typically deal with physical products and services. An emerging trend is the trading of high-valued categories of the cognitive assets that are KIAs. KIAs constitute a large, growing, and influential trading category of goods, the value and transactional volume of which are potentially orders of magnitude larger in monetary value than most consumer goods. KIAs include transactional data, master data, IoT data, data insights and models, digital twins, engineering bills of material, engineering designs and models, courseware, training manuals, diagnostic tools, and even digital assets like NFTs, music, videos, movies, and games.

The market value for transactional and IoT data alone could be more than $50 trillion, based on reports from McKinsey[33], Forrester, Capgemini[34], and other leading business analysts. The fast-growing fields of digital twins, NFTs, games, and music multiply these figures. Effective monetization of KIAs offers the next wave of online marketplace growth, which offers its own promises and challenges.

---

33 https://www.mckinsey.com/~/media/McKinsey/Business%20Functions/McKinsey%20Digital/Our%20Insights/The%20Internet%20of%20Things%20How%20to%20capture%20the%20value%20of%20IoT/How-to-capture-the-value-of-IoT.pdf

34 iot_monetization_0.pdf (capgemini.com)

Data Sets

Among the KIAs listed above, data sets and their derivatives seem to be the most dominant and fastest-growing assets. The value of data and data-driven decision-making is currently well understood. Sharing and monetizing the same data sets has triggered a new opportunity for business growth and new applications. Data sets from one domain have found use across entirely separate industries. An illustrative example is the use of "driving data" now keenly sought by auto insurance companies. This data gathered from technology-connected cars combined with data from other sources, such as weather, events, traffic incidents, and electric vehicle (EV) charging, can be utilized to create a rich ecosystem of valuable information, which has found novel applications and offers tremendous business advantage. Another example is that of banks and financial institutions that use social data collected by Yelp to decide on financial investments where social eminence (how well-known a person or organization seeking a loan is) can become a deciding factor.

Many banks spend $5 to $10 million every year to buy external data related to economic conditions, credit histories, and customer profiles. Major enterprises spend hundreds of millions of dollars every year to acquire external data from media, financial transactions, commodity markets, and logistics data analysts, primarily to combine with in-house data to help optimize business operations and start new ventures.

Types of Data Sets

It would be a nearly impossible task to enumerate all the types of data that are generated or consumed across the world. For instance, a new space data exchange was launched in 2022 by the French space agency Centre National d'Etudes Spatiales (CNES) to encourage development of use cases with various societal and technological impacts, which indicates the broad scope of domains of interest for commercial or scientific usage. The following paragraphs cover a list of major data sets based on their value, volume, and diversity of usage.

Based on the nature of its origin, data can be differentiated into a few major categories, such as transactional data, reference data, master data, and streaming data. In addition, data about data (metadata) is also an important type of information that makes related data comprehensible and usable. The key categories of data are described in more detail below.

Transactional Data

Transactional data is probably the most familiar and popular type of data set and can be categorized as sales data, reservation data, and payments data. Transactional data is information that records an exchange, agreement, or transfer of an entity or service between organizations or individuals. Often, these data sets have commercial and legal implications and are annotated by the time and place of transactions and the parties involved. Examples are sales transactions, event or travel seat reservations, the registering or signing of contracts or documents, loan and bill payments, certificate issuances, granting of entrance admission rights, awarding of prizes, and vote processing. Computing machines have emerged to automate and speed up these transactions, as well as the processing (tabulating, arranging, and analyzing) of associated transactional data.

Reference Data

Reference data are sets of values or classification schemas that are referred to by systems, applications, data stores, processes, and reports, as well as by transactional and master records. Examples include lists of valid values, codes, state abbreviations, demographic fields, flags, product types, genders, charts of account, and product hierarchies.

Reference data sets are also defined by external groups, such as government or regulatory bodies, and are used by multiple organizations. For example, currency codes are defined and maintained by the International Organization for Standardization (ISO).

Master Data

Master data describes the people, places, and things that are involved in an organization's business. Examples include people (customers, employees, vendors, suppliers), places (locations, sales territories, offices), and things (accounts, products, assets, document sets). This data may be used in different transactions and applications and can be considered as relatively static, although updates are always allowed. The main objective of collecting, storing, and maintaining such data is to have a single source usable across the organization. In fact, this is part of the "crown jewel" data of any organization, which has significant business value and needs to be securely stored and used.

Streaming/Measured Data

The streaming data, or Internet of Things (IoT) data, is a fast-emerging category that is assuming greater significance in terms of volume and value. IDC predicts that by 2025[35], the amount of data generated by IoT devices is expected to reach 73.1 ZB (zettabytes).

35 IDC forecasts connected IoT devices to generate 79.4ZB of data in 2025 - FutureIoT

Synthetic Data

Synthetic data is an emerging category of data and is a good example of using AI to help data scientists. The need for large amounts of good data for any kind of AI work can't be overemphasized. Many AI modelers and researchers encounter this issue. If an AI is attempting to create a complex artificial-reasoning entity, why not apply it to generate data as well to help data scientists?

Synthetic data is annotated information that computer simulations or algorithms generate as an alternative to real-world data. In other words, synthetic data is created in digital worlds rather than collected from or measured in the real world. It may be artificial, but synthetic data reflects real-world data, mathematically or statistically. Research demonstrates that, for training an AI model, it can be as good as or even better than data based on actual objects, events, or people. In a June 2021 report on synthetic data, Gartner predicted that by 2030, most of the data used in AI will be artificially generated by rules, statistical models, simulations, or other techniques.

The motivations for synthetic data are many:

- Real data is incomplete: AI needs both large and diverse data sets, but real data is often incomplete, excluding infrequent scenarios that are critical for AI performance.
- Real data is expensive: It's hard to collect, integrate, store, and maintain.
- Real data is biased: Even if data perfectly reflects reality, it can encode biases present in the real world that need to be removed.
- Real data is restricted: Regulation is increasingly limiting data use for AI.

Synthetic data is poised to be a major source of data, even for trading on data marketplaces, and there are already a dozen synthetic data providers in several domains. The Synthetic Data Vault (SDV) is a synthetic data-generation ecosystem of libraries that enables users to easily learn single-table, multi-table, and time series data sets to later generate new synthetic data that has the same format and statistical properties as the original data set.

Metadata

Metadata is data about data. Metadata is closely linked to the data it describes. It's an important part of any data, without which the real data will often be obscure and useless. Users need to understand the data to make the best use of it. The more metadata and context that the data has, the better its use can be. Metadata can include all relevant information of the real data instances, such as descriptions of the schema, the data's lineage, the relationships between pieces, and the data's reliability, quality, and intended use.

Health Care Data

An ecosystem of health care data can lead to more efficient treatment evaluations, provide real-world evidence to determine drug efficacy, support individualized patient journeys, and help identify personal disease risks. However, protecting patient interests and privacy are major challenges in effectively making use of health care data. Data users must adhere to governmental regulations like the Health Insurance Portability and Accountability Act of 1996 (HIPAA).

Health care data can be of different types, such as:

- Patient clinical data

- Patient lab data and imaging data

- Drug data

- Health insurance data

- Medical research data

Data Set Providers

Data is produced and owned by a multitude of sources—persons, organizations, and nature —in general. The primary challenge is how to discover, collect, curate, use, and possibly share the data easily and effectively.

Commercial data suppliers are listed below. Some of these providers are owners themselves, and some of them are data brokers or resellers.

A quick search of data suppliers showed more than 700 commercial suppliers of data in several domains, such as:

- Health care

- Transportation and logistics

- Media

- Supply chain

- Sales and commerce

- Finance, banking, and insurance

- Human resources

- Space and ocean data

- Natural resources

- Government and infrastructure
- Sports and entertainment

While an exhaustive listing of all suppliers is out of the scope of this book, a few major data suppliers and data repositories are:

- Dun & Bradstreet (D&B)
- Bloomberg
- Yelp
- Visa and MasterCard
- www.us.gov
- Google
- Kaggle
- ImageNet
- CodeNet

Data Economy

According to a recent report by Statista, the big data market value (please see the figure) is expected to surpass $100 billion by 2027[36].

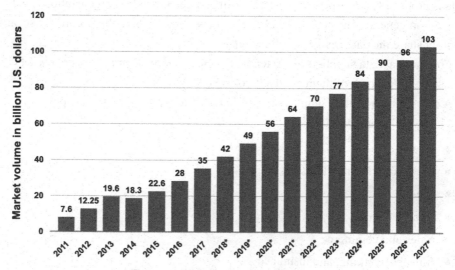

Figure 4.1: Data Economy Growth

36   https://www.statista.com/statistics/254266/global-big-data-market-forecast/

Data Marketplaces

Major data and AI companies such as Google, Amazon, and Snowflake have already launched different types of data marketplaces.

The Snowflake Marketplace[37] was launched in 2019 and offers more than 100 data products. The platform also provides data analytics and data storage functions.

Amazon has recently announced its AWS Data Exchange[38], with several data sets available from both public data suppliers and commercial data vendors.

Google has deployed a new Dataset Search Engine[39], which is currently a free service targeted for the research community and enables cataloging of data made publicly available by data owners.

Oracle also has a well-established data marketplace with B2B data providers.

IBM's Red Hat Marketplace[40] provides data sets and related assets. IBM's Data Asset eXchange (DAX) is another open data source.

Several data repositories, such as Kaggle[41] and the federal government's open data repository (data.gov)[42], are providers of governmental, social, political, and geographic data.

Terbine[43] brings together and contextualizes sensor-generated IoT data sourced from infrastructure and the planet itself. Data feeds from around the globe can be accessed easily via a single interface without having to create thousands of accounts with individual data sources. Terbine obtains data sets consisting of sensor information from a wide variety of sources, including various government agencies, universities, and corporations throughout the world. The data types include aerospace, automotive, energy, logistics, and transportation, as well as many other sectors. More than 34,000 data feeds contribute to the platform.

IOTA[44] and its data marketplace initiative were set up in 2017, with the main objectives of producing an initial, open-source proof of concept (PoC) and exploring new IoT and machine-to-machine (M2M) solutions and business models for the "Economy of Things" (the concept that IoT can potentially turn physical assets

---

37   https://www.snowflake.com/data-marketplace/

38   https://aws.amazon.com/data-exchange/

39   https://datasetsearch.research.google.com/

40   https://marketplace.redhat.com/en-us

41   https://www.kaggle.com/datasets

42   https://www.data.gov/

43   https://terbine.com/

44   https://data.iota.org/#/demo

into participants in global digital markets) to create an ecosystem that can foster permissionless innovation. The participants in the PoC, numbering more than 80 as of January 2019, came from many sectors, including mobility, energy, agriculture, real estate, e-health, smart manufacturing, supply chain, financial services, semiconductors, IT integrators, consulting, universities, and industry clusters.

i3systems[45] is a commercial entity created to develop and launch a commercial IoT marketplace based on an open-source implementation. i3systems has undertaken the task of creating an industrialized version of the i3 open-source software, complete with all the features and support that would be expected of any commercialized software. Recent projects by i3systems include applications related to smart parking, community security, community health care, and video analytics for service-demand planning.

AWS IoT Core[46] also makes it easy to use AWS and Amazon services—such as AWS Lambda, Amazon Kinesis, Amazon S3, Amazon SageMaker, Amazon DynamoDB, Amazon CloudWatch, AWS CloudTrail, Amazon QuickSight, and Alexa Voice Service—to build IoT applications that gather, process, analyze, and act on data generated by connected devices, without having to manage any infrastructure. AWS IoT Core enables connection of any number of devices to the cloud and to other devices without requiring users to provision or manage servers. AWS IoT Core also enables users to scale their device fleets easily and reliably. There are more than 120 IoT partners in the AWS IoT ecosystem.

AI Models

AI applications are becoming pervasive across a wide variety of industry sectors, such as health care, transportation, manufacturing, supply chain, e-commerce, government, customer support, and travel and tourism.

The advent of abundant data has resulted in the proliferation of AI models and their suppliers. Imagine the following scenarios:

- Avid gardeners could create models to recognize different types of roses by simply using their deep knowledge and photographing different rose flowers of wide variety.

- Agronomists could build models that detect potential defects or diseases in agricultural products.

---

45   https://i3-iot.com/what-i3-does/
46   https://aws.amazon.com/iot-core/?nc=sn&loc=2&dn=3

- Classical dancers could build a tutoring model about various facial expressions and hand gestures to teach which are wrong and right.

- Investment analysts could build models to advise which stock to buy or sell based on their experiential knowledge.

- Political strategists could build models based on their knowledge of effects of political headwinds, tailwinds, changing demographics, and opinion poll data.

- Schoolteachers could build models to give the right kind of problems and exercises based on the grade of their students and the students' current levels of performance.

- Pharmacologists could build models to determine which compositions of medicines to stock based on factors such as season and customer demands.

- Oncologists could create models to detect only specific types of cancer.

When it comes to industrial applications, because of the emergence of edge computing, there is a huge potential for the development of "tiny AI" models[47]. These tiny AI models based on simple hardware-embedded or mobile phones may proliferate due to the automation of specific jobs, such as monitoring temperatures and flows, recognizing breaking news, and identifying a specific object, color, or shape. Imagine the number of specialties of science and engineering and the crowdsourcing of such tiny AI models that could be offered free or for a nominal price like mobile apps today. TensorFlow Lite (an open-source software library for ML apps) tool types may enable dedicated AI models to reside in tens of billions of edge devices.

These examples of AI applications reflect a revolution in intelligent apps, especially "semi-professional" videos, music, and training sessions, which can be created and published in forums such as YouTube[48] and TikTok by amateur practitioners. These are not examples of enterprise-level knowledge engineering, developmental efforts, or even professional deployments.

Why is such democratization of AI models only now becoming a reality, although AI researchers have been talking about expert system[49] shells[50,51] for decades? There are two major apparent factors. First, there are now user-friendly and easily accessible

47 https://www.technologyreview.com/technology/tiny-ai/

48 https://www.youtube.com/watch?v=Wuq2aP5O5Z0

49 https://onlinelibrary.wiley.com/doi/10.1111/j.1468-0394.1990.tb00158.x

50 https://en.wikibooks.org/wiki/Expert_Systems/Shells

51 https://www.amazon.com/Developing-Knowledge-Based-Systems-Expert-System/dp/0023818751

tools to build them; it's long been a dream of AI developers to have "shells" that can be used to build apps with rich contents. Second, there is now an abundance of data created and made available in electronic form by practicing experts. It isn't difficult at all for amateur botanists to take thousands of pictures and upload them into an image database for creating a model by themselves.

An explosion of AI models can be expected soon in narrow application areas—both professional and consumer fields. This points to the emerging problem of managing AI model tasks, such as cataloging, categorizing, qualifying, and standardizing as well as monetizing these assets appropriately.

However, the current scenario is a good example of missing industry standards, trust, and transparency of models, mostly due to a variety of amateur players. Lack of interface standardization often leads to difficulties for application-integration teams. The big AI companies (e.g., IBM, Microsoft, Google) are focusing on their internal assets, which are primarily aimed at their enterprise customers. The current lack of interoperability standards severely limits the opportunities to adapt and integrate existing models or to build larger applications. Interestingly, almost all current AI marketplaces have few models—that is, no more than 50 models—which demonstrates the currently nascent stage of this business.

There are some efforts underway to recommend and promote industry standards for AI interoperability and trustworthiness, such as those of IEEE,[52] Responsible Artificial Intelligence Institute[53], and few other organizations.

There is a strong need to have a well-managed platform and a consolidated effort[54] to enforce standards, security, and trust of core AI APIs and component models, like the Google App and Apple App stores for common mobile APIs. While the app stores of Google and Apple have more than two million applications in each of their inventories, the percentage of AI apps is low. Liability, trustworthiness, security, and above all the lineage of AI models are of critical consideration during a marketplace sale transaction.

Types of AI Models

AI models and model-embedded applications are numerous and span all sorts of sectors, such as:

---

52   https://standards.ieee.org/ieee/2941.1/10567/
53   https://www.responsible.ai/
54   Marketplace for AI Models (arxiv.org)

- Health care (preventive care, causal reasoning models, diagnosis, therapy recommendation, medical research like DNA sequencing, and root-cause analysis)
- Pharma (drug discovery, impact analysis)
- Transportation (routing, scheduling, pricing)
- Supply chain (procurement risk estimation, routing, optimal inventory management)
- Finance and banking (risk estimation, investment recommendation, revenue prediction, business-decision optimization, 360-degree analysis)
- Trading and retail (recommendation, personalization, customer segmentation, optimal pricing, revenue predictions, and incentive and rebate management)
- Human resources (employee recruiting, resume analysis, employee evaluation and compensation recommendations, retention and attrition predictions, and HR capacity predictions)
- Intelligent interfaces (natural language models, speech synthesis models, speech generation, and language translation).

AI Model Suppliers and Consumers

An AI model market is emerging with a few active players. A way to group these players is as hyperscalers, ISVs, and specialty model providers.

Hyperscalers build ecosystems of AI models, tools, and services to promote their cloud platforms. Examples include AWS Marketplace, Azure Marketplace, GCP Marketplace, and IBM Cloud.

ISV platforms are AI platform providers with partner solutions. Examples include C3 AI, Modzy, Cloud28+ (HPE), Acumos, BigML, Red Hat Marketplace, and IBM Cloud Pak for Data.

Specialty players are niche marketplaces targeting specific use cases, industry, and consortia. Examples include OVH (SaaS), ModelDepot (Image/Text), Nuance, Modelplace.AI, and Singularity.AI. Specialty players offer models in niche industry areas, such as weather forecasting, career advising, and specialty health care.

AI Economy

General use cases of AI models and applications are well documented, although new and innovative applications are always emerging in previously unimagined areas. According to a recent McKinsey Report, the adoption of AI has been steadily increasing among different sectors of AI, predominantly in the high tech and telecom industries[55].

International Data Corporation (IDC) estimates that the worldwide AI market, including software, hardware, and services, will post a compound annual growth rate (CAGR) of 18.6 percent in the 2022–2026 period and will reach the $900 billion mark in 2026[56].

AI Marketplace Players

AI marketplaces are still in a nascent stage; however, both small and big players are testing the market already. While some of the tech players like Microsoft and IBM are showcasing their AI tools and APIs on their cloud platforms, there are startup companies that are focusing on domain-specific and application-oriented models.

The marketplaces can be categorized as follows:

- Hyperscalers, such as AWS, Azure, and Google[57], which provide a comprehensive set of services in their marketplace, including AI and ML as a subcategory. The AI services offered in these marketplaces usually go along with the corresponding hyperscale platform.

- ISV platforms, such as IBM Cloud and Red Hat, which provide a comprehensive set of services in their marketplace, including AI and ML as a subcategory. The AI services offered in these marketplaces usually go along with the corresponding hybrid cloud architecture.

- AI-focused ISV platforms, such as C3 AI and Modzy, which provide AI capabilities that are offered as SaaS or on-premises platforms.

- AI model marketplaces, such as Singularity, which are focused on AI models.

- Specialty marketplaces, such as Bonseyes, Clearhead, Nuance, and Modelplace. AI, which focus on specific tasks such as matching data scientists with innovators and diagnostic imaging.

55 https://www.mckinsey.com/business-functions/mckinsey-analytics/our-insights/global-survey-the-state-of-ai-in-2020

56 https://www.idc.com/getdoc.jsp?containerId=prEUR249536522

57 https://console.cloud.google.com/marketplace/details/google-cloud-platform/cloud-machine-learning-engine?pli=1

Categorization of AI Marketplaces

- AWS [58]: A comprehensive marketplace, with more than 900 offerings under an ML category. Approximately 50 percent of the offerings are for the AWS SageMaker platform.

- Microsoft Azure: A comprehensive marketplace with more than 1,500 offerings under an AI + ML category. Most of the offerings are from third parties, mostly as SaaS.

- Google Cloud Marketplace[59],: Google Cloud offers more than 250 offerings if searched for AI.

- Red Hat Marketplace: This marketplace includes an AI/ML category with more than 25 offerings from IBM and third-party vendors.

- Modzy[60]: A ModelOps and MLOps platform with third-party models included, offered as SaaS or on-premises.

- Modelplace.AI: A specialty model marketplace with out-of-the-box models that handle in-browser testing and API integration.

- Hugging Face: A model marketplace plus an ecosystem. This community of AI model builders offers a large collection (more than 30,000) of high-quality ML models.

- Algorithmia: A commercial MLOps platform that enables companies to deploy models from various frameworks and make them available for consumption. Customers can deploy using SaaS, hosting, or on-premises.

- Clearhead: A specialty (SaaS model) alpha-launched marketplace that is purely a SaaS deployment model. The applications are exposed as an API.

- Nuance AI Marketplace: Offers specialty imaging models and a marketplace for diagnostic imaging, which brings AI directly into a radiology workflow. It gives radiologists a convenient, one-stop shop to select, prove, and execute AI in their workflows, bridging the technology divide to make AI useful, usable, and used. Nuance claims to be the industry's first workflow-integrated market for diagnostic-imaging AI algorithms.

---

58 https://aws.amazon.com/marketplace/solutions/machine-learning

59 https://console.cloud.google.com/marketplace/details/google-cloud-platform/cloud-machine-learning-engine?pli=1

60 https://www.modzy.com/platform/ai-model-marketplace/

- C3 AI: A marketplace and tools provider that offers a comprehensive enterprise-targeted platform for AI consumption. The marketplace enables publishers to list their models. The company claims a significant number of current customers.

- BigML: Provides a suite of algorithms (not called models) (supervised and unsupervised learning algorithms) with which users can design their own models. Available as SaaS or on-premises as subscription.

- SeeMe.ai[61]: A platform, a framework, and tools that let users create, manage, and enhance data sets; train, test, and deploy models; and share the data sets and models for private or public access and consumption. The platform enables performance of several data set transformation tasks, annotations, labeling, and browsing actions. The platform also supports AI model lifecycle management. SeeMe.ai appears to be intended for the developer and modeler ecosystem rather than being an asset-trading platform.

- Bonseyes[62]: A collaborative community of entrepreneurs, researchers, investors, regulators, and citizens. It supports building AI solutions for industries. Bonseyes provides access to advanced tools and services obtainable via a marketplace ecosystem of leading academic and industrial partners. The focus of Bonseyes is on Edge AI. It has an "AI Lab" for creating AI applications and an AI marketplace to commercialize the models.

AI Models as a Service

Model as a Service (MaaS) is a concept in which the customers don't purchase a copy for their exclusive use and deployment, but instead use a model to obtain results of inferencing for a given set of data. This amounts to a nonexclusive subscription model in which the users either pay as they go or pay a periodic subscription fee, depending on the resources needed and types of usage. This is an unusual business model, especially in a public cloud environment, and it's more common on the software tool side, such as in Microsoft Office on the cloud, Google Cloud services, and IBM Bluemix.

AI Foundation Models as a Service

The emergence of powerful AI foundation models offers an opportunity to provide services users can employ to develop application models that can be more powerful and

---

61   https://www.seeme.ai/
62   https://www.bonseyes.eu/

robust than traditional deep-learning models built from the ground up. A foundation model[63] is defined as any model that is trained on broad data at scale and can be adapted (fine-tuned or using in-context learning) to a wide range of downstream tasks and applications. The AI foundation models are a paradigm shift and one of the main topics of discussion in the industry. Foundation models are not something new. These are models like BERT, RoBERTa, T5, BART, GPT-3/4, CLIP, DALL·E, and Codex.

A foundation model can centralize information from all data taken from various modalities. This basic model can then be adapted to a wide range of downstream tasks. Data is naturally multi-modal in some domains—for example, medical images, structured data, and clinical text in health care. Thus, multi-modal foundation models are a natural way of fusing all the relevant information about a domain and adapting to tasks that also span multiple modes. With self-supervised training, foundation models can scale much better than supervised training, because it's much easier to obtain more unlabeled than labeled data. Also, a model can potentially learn more expressive representation because it's richer than the more limited label space of supervised data.

There are five key properties of a foundation model:

- Expressivity—To flexibly capture and represent rich information
- Scalability—To efficiently consume large quantities of data
- Multimodality—To connect various modalities and domains
- Memory capacity—To store the vast amount of accumulated knowledge
- Compositionality—To generalize to new contexts, tasks, and environments

It's amazing to note the rapid scaling up of these massive models as the recent announcement of PaLM[64],[65] by Google (which has an approximately 570 billion parameter network) shows.

The emerging AI foundational models can be seen as a basis of a service offered on platforms, which can be used by domain experts to build application-specific models without the trouble of handling massive amounts of data.

Issues Specific to AI Marketplaces

AI models as a trading commodity bring additional issues and concerns into the marketplace domain. The issues of privacy, bias, security, and drift are widely

---

63 https://arxiv.org/pdf/2108.07258.pdf

64 https://storage.googleapis.com/pathways-language-model/PaLM-paper.pdf

65 https://ai.googleblog.com/2022/04/pathways-language-model-palm-scaling-to.html

discussed in the AI industry. The same issues are amplified and become more serious when it comes to the sale of these models via a marketplace.

Kush Varshney[66] rightly points out that "accuracy is not enough when you are developing machine learning systems. You also need to make sure that your models are fair, have not been tampered with, will not fall apart in different conditions, and can be understood by people."

Trustworthiness of AI Models

Trustworthiness of AI models is a basic requirement for acceptability of such models for applications, especially for critical ones like health care, autonomous navigation, and robotics. Commercial transactions that involve AI models have the added responsibility of making sure that the models on the platform are trustworthy. The trustworthiness depends on many factors, such as the source and lineage of the data, the accuracy and correctness of the solutions and inferences, and model development.

Lineage is an important factor in ensuring trustworthiness. It amounts to the transparency and metadata about the model, such as what methodology was used to build the model, what level or types of testing have been done, what the source of the data is, which version of the data is behind each of the versions of the models, when the model was built and updated, and who built the model.

The accuracy of models is an obvious criterion. However, sometimes there is an overemphasis on the percentage of accuracy because of academic competition in marginally improved performances, which often ignores the cost of computation. It's often claimed that a couple of points of increase in accuracy warrants significantly larger computing power, in the face of which one has to decide what is an acceptable level of accuracy based on a cost-benefit analysis. More importantly, a model should record this information as part of its metadata and documentation. The level of accuracy required also depends on the type of application and the use-case context.

The ability to explain how the AI model arrived at a solution is an important aspect of instilling trust and acceptance of the model. As with human experts who must explain the rationale behind the decision or inference they're making, the AI models also need to provide the reasoning and methodology behind the expert recommendation, decision, or answer provided. The deep-learning models are, in general, weak in providing satisfactory explanations other than the fact that a conclusion has been based on the patterns of the data on which the models were trained. Explainability of AI models is an advantageous feature for commercializing

66 http://www.trustworthymachinelearning.com/

hem, and there is an increased interest in developing new approaches, such as neuro-symbolic models and causal models, in order to support better explainability of AI models.

Regulatory Compliance and Liability Issues

Many countries, such as Canada, China, India, UK, and the European Union, have created policies and regulations[67] to ensure the powerful AI technology is used properly without causing damage or distress to the human community and surrounding ecosystems. All AI model developers and vendors are expected to "certify" their models to make sure they conform to local regulations.

Any potential damage, even if inadvertently caused, can be a liability issue. This becomes even more important if the model is employed for sensitive areas like fraud detection, medical diagnosis, fault detection, or credit assessment. It's still unclear who has the responsibility for the model, whether it should be the providers of the data for models, algorithm designers, model developers, or application owners. There is also a potential danger of opening a plethora of legal battles as AI models become widespread, especially when commercially sold to end users. This could be the most serious impediment for wide-scale commercial exchange of AI models.

Recently, the Federal Trade Commission (FTC) proposed guidelines concerning the regulation of AI. The FTC blog post[68] basically recommends that those who use or license AI in a way that affects consumer well-being must do so in a manner that is "transparent," particularly regarding decisions that affect a consumer's credit. As such, many of the decisions concerning the use and implementation of AI in the consumer context can be regulated by Section (5)(a) of the FTC Act, which provides that "unfair or deceptive acts or practices in or affecting commerce are declared unlawful."

The EU has published a guide called "Liability for Artificial Intelligence and other emerging digital technologies"[69]. It says that an AI application's rollout must come with sufficient safeguards to minimize the risk of consequences these technologies may cause, such as bodily injury or other harm. In the EU, product safety regulations ensure this is the case. However, such regulations cannot completely exclude the possibility of damage resulting from the operation of these technologies. If this happens, victims will seek compensation.

---

67 https://en.wikipedia.org/wiki/Regulation_of_artificial_intelligence
68 https://www.ftc.gov/business-guidance/blog/2020/04/using-artificial-intelligence-algorithms
69 https://op.europa.eu/en/publication-detail/-/publication/1c5e30be-1197-11ea-8c1f-01aa75ed71a1/language-en

Interoperability

For AI marketplaces to be successful, there needs to be a standard format for model interfaces and connected workflows. This standard would enable developers to implement diverse technology tools without being locked into a particular framework or vendor. The multiplicity of technology formats makes it difficult for AI systems to work together and causes companies to waste cycles of developer hours to translate between frameworks. For this reason, in September 2017, Facebook and Microsoft introduced a system for switching between ML frameworks, such as PyTorch and Caffe2, to create an open ecosystem for AI model interoperability[70].

Security of AI Models

As enterprise-grade AI models are deployed in hybrid multi-cloud environments, "zero trust" has become a major motivation for building secure and attack-resilient AI models. Business stakeholders need access to data and the ability to perform AI computing in zero trust environments, even as they retain complete control over the security of their data and intellectual property (IP) and have absolute guarantees against leakage. Using AI models that are resilient to evasion, poisoning, model theft, and data leakage attacks while concurrently leveraging data across the enterprise has become a top priority for AI practitioners.

IBM, as well as the larger technical community, is pursuing two broad directions in AI model security innovations. Capabilities that can help build resilient AI solutions are starting to emerge. One area of thrust is in building resilience within the AI model with its metadata. For example, research in adversarial robustness is addressing robustness against evasion, poisoning, model theft, and data-leakage attacks. A second area of pursuit is the development of metadata tagging (e.g., fact sheets), which captures results of a readiness evaluation exercise that grades the AI model on its resilience against adversarial attacks[71].

Power Demand

Researchers at the University of Massachusetts Amherst[72] estimated the energy cost of developing AI language models by measuring the power consumption of common hardware used during training. They found that training BERT just once has the carbon

70   https://azure.microsoft.com/en-us/blog/microsoft-and-facebook-create-open-ecosystem-for-ai-model-interoperability/

71   https://researcher.watson.ibm.com/researcher/view_group.php?id=9571

72   https://arxiv.org/pdf/1906.02243.pdf

footprint of a passenger flying round trip between New York and San Francisco. It is highly recommended to have a concerted effort by industry and academia to promote research of more computationally efficient algorithms, as well as hardware that requires less energy. Wasting energy for marginally better results may not be desirable.

Ethical Usage of AI Models

From an AI marketplace perspective, the application use-case types and who uses them also matter. The more powerful tools and assets are, the chances of them reaching the wrong hands and being employed for the wrong purposes are also higher. The ethical use of AI is a much-discussed topic even in nontechnical forums. For example, social scientists, politicians, and human rights activists are all concerned about the ethical usage of AI models. When a marketplace tries to sell or exchange such intelligent tools, the concern is about bias and potential damage to humans and nature in general. The marketplace needs to ensure proper checks and controls to ensure that the AI models and tools are being used in ethical ways. This is often controlled by regulations being rolled out in many countries.

Application Program Interfaces (APIs)

The rapid growth of mobile applications and cloud platforms has accelerated the explosion of APIs for different functions. Gone are the days when teams developed all pieces of code by themselves. Developers often assemble an application using compossible components. APIs enable companies to more easily construct products and services that could otherwise take too long to build[73]. The demand for reusable APIs is becoming more and more irrelevant not only because the ready-to-use APIs make lab-to-market quicker, but also because of the important benefit of interoperability and standardization.

APIs enable different systems to talk to each other using a seamless standard interface that enables building of applications much more quickly and easily. Several good examples of APIs have evolved in the areas of finance, B2B commerce, graphics, database access, search, and navigation. One of the reasons for API influence in application development is the secular growth in cloud computing, which has led to the need for integration. Another important driving factor is the emergence of proliferating mobile applications, which require several building blocks for interface control, data access, and communication between multiple data sources and application servers.

---

73   https://www.forbes.com/sites/tomtaulli/2020/01/18/api-economy--is-it-the-next-big-thing/#6f28b4c242ff

Types of APIs

In many cases, commercial APIs can be classified as application-specific or domain-specific. The latter type is the more generic utility (or core API) useful in a wider variety of domains.

Because there are hundreds of thousands of commercially available APIs, certain prominent categories and application domains are mentioned here only as representative examples. It's interesting to note that many popular service providers have started exposing APIs to enable access to their applications by other businesses and application developers. For example, the Google Maps API lets other companies use it in their maps, without requiring those companies to build their own system. A Slack API enables applications to integrate within that messaging platform. An UberEats API enables businesses to deliver food to customers without launching their own service. PayPal, Visa, and Mastercard companies offer their APIs for companies and establishments to facilitate money payments. Weather companies like IBM's The Weather Company offer APIs to make weather information accessible to consumers and other businesses. While some of these APIs are priced, others are offered free in the common interest, albeit with a reduced set of functionalities.

API Providers and Consumers

There are already many marketplaces that handle transactional APIs. Some examples are Celigo[74], Plaid[75], Zymr[76], Rapid API[77], API Connect[78], Rakuten[79], Prompt API[80], Twilio[81], Yappes[82], and Akana[83].

74   https://www.celigo.com/

75   https://plaid.com/

76   https://www.zymr.com/ecosystem-connectors/

77   https://rapidapi.com/

78   https://www.cloudfoundry.org/the-foundry/api-connect/

79   https://developers.rakuten.com/

80   https://promptapi.com/provider

81   https://www.twilio.com/

82   https://yappes.com/

83   https://www.akana.com/products/api-platform

API Economy

The API economy is a business model built around the use of APIs in the digital economy[84]. Developers from industries including financial services, telecommunications, and health care are showing strong and fast-growing interest in monetizing APIs. Standardized and reusable APIs that can offer uses in a wide variety of applications make the APIs a major source of tradeable and monetizable assets. Best examples are navigation APIs from Google, weather forecast APIs, and currency conversion APIs.

According to some market research studies, the global market for APIs is around $2.5 billion today and is expected to grow to $6 to $10 billion by 2028.[85].

The 2019 acquisition by Salesforce.com of MuleSoft (a management system for APIs) for $6.5 billion and Visa's purchase of Plaid for $5.3 billion are ample evidence of the growing API market economy.

API Marketplaces and Playgrounds

APIs provide a much-needed abstraction of the low-level details and complexities in implementing common functions. APIs are important components of all software development projects, especially those enabling communication between systems and applications, accessing data, and creating transactions. One of the interesting facts about APIs is that the producers and consumers of APIs belong to the same developer community. Facilitating an ecosystem in which developers can try out APIs before they decide to buy or use them, as well as enabling them to experiment and develop new APIs on the same platform—often by modifying, extending, or combining existing APIs—is critical to the nurturing of the API marketplace. Industry is calling this ecosystem an "API playground for developers."

An API playground needs to have features such as trial versions of APIs, sample data with which to test APIs, sample applications, example code, development and test tools, and user-interface templates. APIs belong to domain-specific professionals and application developers, so a simple showcasing is not sufficient to convince all consumers[86]. At the same time, seasoned developers understand which APIs are needed by the community and realize they could develop those APIs on a platform where they can also communicate, interact, and collaborate with fellow developers, as well as

84   https://www.akana.com/blog/api-economy
85   https://www.prnewswire.com/news-releases/global-api-management-market-to-be-worth-usd-6263-million-by-2028-with-cagr-of-11-3---zion-market-research-301377394.html
86   https://wilsonmar.github.io/api-ecosystem/

monetize the APIs. Most API marketplaces make such playgrounds an integral part of their platforms.

Software Modules

Software is a product that is most naturally amenable for digital-trading platforms and is a dominant KIA. This market was originally dominated by big industry players like Microsoft, IBM, SAP, and Oracle, which used their own e-commerce portals to offer their software products and "evolutionize" those same assets as a service— famously known as Software as a Service (SaaS) platforms. The market was and is still dominated by B2B and some B2C sales companies that often sell their own products on their own platforms. Many marketplaces report that software transactions mostly happen as private sales, for which supplier-buyer discussions, negotiations, and demos happen outside the platform. In such cases, the marketplace platform acts as a lead generator and, in some cases, the transaction executor as well.

Software Marketplaces

Software products are probably the oldest members of the KIA product suite. Major tech companies and IT houses have been selling software products via their own marketplaces for years. One of the main reasons for selling software via online marketplaces is the fact that this process is much better understood and easier to use than those of other KIA assets.

Digital Twins

A digital twin (DT) is a digital representation of a physical object or system. A DT is a virtual representation of an object or system that spans its lifecycle, is updated from real-time data, and uses simulation, machine learning, and reasoning to help in decision-making. The technology behind digital twins has expanded to include large items such as buildings, factories, and even cities. In the future, people and processes could also have digital twins, expanding the concept further. The idea first arose at NASA, which created full-scale mockups of early space capsules, which it used on the ground to mirror and diagnose problems in orbit. These mockups eventually gave way to fully digital simulations.

A DT is constructed so it can receive input from sensors gathering data from a real-world counterpart. This enables the DT to simulate the physical object in real time and, in the process, offer insights into performance and potential problems. The DT could also be designed based on a prototype of its physical counterpart, in which case the twin can provide feedback as the product is refined. A twin could even serve as a prototype itself before any physical version is built.

According to the latest analysis by Emergen Research, the global DT market is expected to reach $106.26 billion by 2028[87].

Types of AI Digital Twins

DTs can be built to simulate any physical system, process, or device/equipment. Industry specifies the following categories of DTs:

- Equipment
- Component
- Process
- Biological

Equipment DTs

An equipment DT is a digital simulation of a machine or piece of equipment that fully mimics the original's functional behavior (except its wear and tear). With a DT, an operator can train on a virtual machine, thereby eliminating the cost of a dedicated trainer or simulator. Such machines are useful for optimization of operations, failure diagnosis, and what-if analysis of various operating conditions.

Component Twins, Parts Twins, Asset Twins

Component twins are the basic unit of a DT, the smallest example of a functioning component. Parts twins are roughly the same thing but pertain to components of slightly less importance.

When two or more components work together, they form what is known as an asset. Asset twins let observers study the interaction of those components, creating a wealth of performance data that can be processed and turned into actionable insights.[88]

Process DTs

Process digital twins, the macro level of magnification, reveal how systems work together to create an entire production facility. The process DT enhances a product DT

---

87   https://www.emergenresearch.com/blog/top-10-digital-twin-companies-impacting-industry-
        4-0-innovations-in-2021
88   https://www.ibm.com/topics/what-is-a-digital-twin

beyond a single machine to encompass an entire production environment[89]. The process DT uses mixed reality, AI, and high-performance computing to optimize views of not only equipment, but the entire manufacturing process. The streamlined collaboration provided by bridging virtual and physical environments is why the process DT is a new class of DT. Its capabilities not only build on those of a product DT, but also present a new value proposition to the manufacturing world and enable manufacturers to achieve efficiencies and insights not possible before.

Biological DTs

Examples of this type include a DT of the heart (which represents the electrical behavior of the organ for setting up a pacemaker), a DT of the chemical aspect of the heart for drug development, or the mechanical response for surgery simulation. DTs will shift the current treatment selection based on the state of the patient today to an optimized state of the patient of tomorrow[90].

DT Suppliers and Consumers

Commercial DT offerings are being offered by some of the largest industrial equipment companies. General Electric (GE) developed DT technology internally as part of its jet-engine manufacturing process and is now offering its expertise to customers, as is Siemens, another industrial giant heavily involved in manufacturing. IBM is marketing digital twins as part of its IoT push, and Microsoft is offering its own digital-twin platform under the Azure umbrella.

Some of the digital twins are for:

- Automobile engines
- Wind energy generators
- Defense applications—tests and mission-simulation targets
- Oil and minerals (mining and geophysical models)

There are several major companies offering commercial DTs. Microsoft Azure Digital Twins enables users to model environments such as factories, farms, energy networks, buildings, stadiums, railways, and cities by connecting assets like IoT devices to existing business systems. Digital Twins Definition Language (DTDL)

---

89 https://cloudblogs.microsoft.com/industry-blog/manufacturing/2017/10/23/the-process-digital-twin-a-step-toward-operational-excellence/

90 https://www.linkedin.com/pulse/6-digital-twin-applications-healthcare-revolution-enrique/

s used in models to describe twins in terms of their components, state properties, commands, telemetry events, and relationships.

GE has created the most advanced DT, which integrates analytic models for components of a power plant that measure asset health, wear, and conformance with customer-defined Key Performance Indicators (KPIs) to the organization's objectives. GE also offers additional "control knobs" or "dimensionality" to improve the performance of the system or asset modeled with GE Digital Twin.

Siemens has developed and commercialized several DTs and offers Siemens Digital Enterprise, which can digitalize entire value-added processes within different production modules. Another product, MindSphere, helps users develop new digital business models and offers state-of-the-art security functions in the cloud.

Digital Twin as a Service (DTaaS)

DT simulation models can be complex and often require extensive computing resources just to use them. Also, in some situations, a DT is used infrequently by customers, such as once a month or twice a year, in which case it may be too expensive to buy the software for creating a DT because the usage rates are so low. This is the context in which it's relevant to offer DTs as a service via an on-demand business model. The platform owner may deploy the DT as a service, allowing customers to subscribe to that service as and when needed. The monetary model can be time-period based, such as a monthly or yearly subscription, or usage-based, like other SaaS cloud offerings. DT models of large systems and complex equipment are best suited for this business model. Some of the advantages to the supplier are as obvious as those of any other SaaS offering, such as the ability to quickly deploy revisions to the service, a recurring revenue stream, and the ability to gain a better understanding of the types of use cases and workloads the users are employing.

Digital Twin Exchanges

The IBM Digital Twin Exchange[91] is a resource for asset-intensive industries, including organizations managing enterprise-wide digital and physical assets. IBM Digital Twin Exchange provides access to DT data for equipment, facilities, and IoT use. The Digital Twin Exchange enables sharing of DT downloads that make it easier to manage connected assets, equipment, and IoT solutions.

---

91   https://www.ibm.com/docs/en/announcements/digital-twin-exchange?region=US

Bosch IoT Hub[92] offers DT management in a secure way. Bosch IoT Things is based on the open-source project Eclipse Ditto, which helps devices communicate directly and efficiently via an API. It also supports security and common authentication mechanisms, such as usernames or passwords.

Engineering Designs, Drawings, and Manuals

With standardized manufacturing processes in place, commercial exchanges of engineering designs, drawings, and bills of material have become tradeable commodities. This is a fast-emerging area in which several business models are finding their way, such as sale of engineering designs, connecting engineers to manufacturers and suppliers, connecting contracting vendors to consumers (including large engineering firms), recruitment or temporary hiring of engineering professionals, and platforms for bidding for engineering projects. The areas include architectural designs, computer numerical control (CNC) tooling, and 3D printing.

Xometry[93] has unveiled its 2D Technical Drawing Marketplace, a platform to expand access to prospective job orders for 3,000+ American machine shops. A recent industry article[94] states that "53 percent of mechanical engineers worked with parts that lacked 3D Computer-Aided Design (CAD) files, representing a potential $37 billion market. Specifically, these files are often used for legacy parts and in sectors where diminishing manufacturing sources and material shortages issues are common."

Cad Crowd[95] is another example of an engineering design marketplace. The platform offers standard as well as custom CAD designs, connects with contractors, and checks the quality of engineering work done. The Cad Crowd platform facilitates hiring prequalified professional CAD designers and 3D modelers with proven expertise and knowledge, and sponsors a design contest in which it reviews submissions from multiple participants.

GrabCAD[96], with the advent of a large pool of talented engineers and abundant engineering assets, has launched a marketplace recently. With its large library of CAD designs, this marketplace connects its engineers with anyone in need of technical drawings and CAD-related services, promising a 24-hour turnaround and a flat fee for

---

92 https://bosch-iot-suite.com/
93 https://www.xometry.com/
94 https://www.digitalengineering247.com/article/xometry-launches-2d-technical-drawing-marketplace/
95 https://www.cadcrowd.com/
96 https://grabcad.com/

all "simple projects." These can be assets such as technical drawings, photo-realistic images, and 3D models. For those commissioning CAD services, the marketplace aims to solve the problem of finding a reliable outsourcing partner and removes hassles related to payments, workflow, and confidentiality. CAD engineers can also offer other skills as services on the platform. However, the broader idea behind GrabCAD is to let CAD engineers share 3D models, solving the problem of them spending too much time designing products or components that already exist elsewhere in the form of drawings. The GrabCAD site's "Request a Model" feature, which lets users place a free "wanted" ad for a particular model or drawing, is proving popular with users asking for help.

Media Entertainment Products

Digital media includes video, audio, artistic works, news, and other entertainment content that is created, edited, stored, or accessed in digital form. The creation and distribution of digital media has already outpaced that of traditional print newspapers, magazines, discs, and tapes in terms of popularity and user-base size. Passionate amateurs can now afford to make and distribute independent movies using digital media without the prohibitive costs of film. The success of publishing platforms like YouTube, Instagram, Apple iTunes, and other exchanges and marketplaces have made the generation, distribution, and monetization of entertainment assets quicker, cheaper, and more massive in numbers. Sophisticated software for recording, editing, and publishing songs, videos, and movies has revolutionized the media industry.

Digital transformation of media has led to many trends like 24x7 availability of content, content on all types of devices, personalized content delivery, and new platforms for advertisements, which are an essential part of any entertainment program[97]. The direct-to-consumer (D2C) streaming of content has opened many promising opportunities, including more massive audiences, reduction of costly and cumbersome traditional distribution channels, and demand-driven content generation. Another interesting development is the democratization of content generation in which sophisticated tools and platforms are now available for any musician, director, or artist—even if they are amateurs—to create, publish, popularize, and monetize quality entertainment products. The role of the entertainment ecosystem platforms in this context has become more of an aggregation of the various contents, enabling cataloging, rating, downloading, and playing these works on the platform.

---

97 https://cloudblogs.microsoft.com/industry-blog/microsoft-in-business/media-comm/2019/04/29/the-future-of-media-entertainment-in-the-experience-economy/

The technological challenges are more complex when it comes to entertainment assets because of the variety of the print, audio, and video contents covering different types of end products, such as music, drama, movies, sports, games, races, gambling, puzzles, and podcasts.

Types of Digital Media Products

Music

Music audios and videos are probably the most popular and predominant digital entertainment products in the market. The advent of online media players has made tapes and CDs obsolete. It was a brilliant business move when Apple announced its iTunes services along with a smartphone app that can play audio and video, which now brings in about $18 billion in annual revenue.

The music market includes classical and live concerts, film music, music albums, instrumentals, and streaming audio. The digitization and ease of online music publishing have brought musicians closer to their audiences and made it possible to share music from all corners of the world. The COVID-related lockdowns and restrictions that prevented live programs particularly have driven the scaling up of online concerts and online musical events.

Videos and Movies

The advent of smartphones and cheaper cameras enabled the creation of high-quality videos as well as the recording of events and programs. Moreover, social media and YouTube have provided additional publishing platforms. These may not directly result in commercialization, but much indirect monetization is happening because of the availability of a large set of videos and the ease of publishing or sharing the videos via many popular platforms.

Some reports give astonishing numbers, such as 720,000 hours of video being uploaded daily onto YouTube alone. YouTube viewers watch approximately one billion hours of video every day. This shows the supply and demand potential for amateur and professional videos on a multitude of topics, such as political, scientific, business, entertainment, and educational.

Just like audio contents, video contents also pose specific challenges, such as privacy, ethical correctness, upload and download speeds, ease of use, and facilities on which to play or run the videos. Interestingly, 62 percent of businesses[98] use YouTube.

---

98   https://www.webfx.com/blog/internet/youtube-marketing-statistics/

As of January 2023, YouTube and Netflix ranked at the top in streaming and providing online TV segments[99].

Many professional music video albums, commercial movies, and short features are published on online platforms today. The global film and video market has reached a value of nearly $100 billion[100] currently.

News and TV Shows

The market size of digital news media is approximately $40 billion. About 20 percent of news consumers use online digital media, and this figure is growing exponentially. Because of the value in real-time reporting, digital print media has a greater advantage over traditional print media, and push technology and mobile platforms enable it to penetrate to a larger audience, especially among younger consumers. Moreover, personalized and focused news delivery is also possible because of technology enablement of online news bulletins.

Media Exchanges/Marketplaces

Media exchanges are probably the largest marketplace platforms in terms of content volume, customer base, and revenue. Netflix, Meta/Facebook, and iTunes have already been described in an earlier chapter. Besides these media industry giants, many traditional entertainment producers and broadcasters have also moved to digital platforms. Some of the communication and content generators have benefited from their specific capabilities—with either networks and data bandwidth or the rich contents they own—to become entertainment media marketplaces. Prime examples are AT&T TV, Bloomberg TV, Disney Plus[101], and NFL+[102], all of which have their own marketplaces that charge subscriptions for live streaming or access to libraries of media products. Additional examples include Amazon TV and Artlist[103].

Digital Media Economy

The global entertainment market is worth more than $2 trillion, and a sizable part of it is in the form of digital online media platforms.

---

99   https://www.enterpriseappstoday.com/stats/media-and-entertainment-industry-statistics.html

100 https://www.grandviewresearch.com/industry-analysis/movies-entertainment-market

101 https://www.disneyplus.com/

102 https://www.nfl.com/videos/

103 https://artlist.io/

PwC is forecasting[104] that this sector will enjoy a 5 percent CAGR that will raise industry revenues to $2.6 trillion in 2025. Within this sector, PwC is forecasting the biggest growth trajectory to be in video streaming, with a projected CAGR of 10.6 percent by 2025, which would make it an $81.3 billion industry.

Games

Gaming is a fast-growing industry, rightly amplified by the recent acquisition of Activision by Microsoft at a record valuation of $68 billion.

The consumer nature of this second most valuable (next only to data) digital asset means its trading and associated services will probably dwarf the values of any entertainment products and many technology products as well. Two interesting factors that make the digital game industry so attractive is solving its technological challenges (graphics, performance speed, and computing demands) to satisfy its primary audience: young and addictive consumers who are willing to pay for often-overpriced games.

The growth of powerful graphics processing units (GPUs) and the high-speed networking possible with 5G has opened a world of gaming platforms that consumers can access from a multitude of devices without owning or being tied to specific gadgets and associated technology. In fact, this growth paves the way to fade the line between gaming and social networks. As one can imagine, the "buddying" in playing together or competing can be a stronger and more influential network than that of Meta/Facebook friends or Instagram followers. The monetization of gaming platforms for social networking and associated ads and other marketing opportunities is yet to bloom fully. Big players like Microsoft, Google, TikTok, and Meta will be eyeing this area as part of their next phase of revenue growth[105].

Mobile gaming itself is estimated to be more than $90 billion and is growing at more than 7 percent annually. Making money through selling skins of entertainment products and gaming currency has further accelerated the business value of the gaming industry[106].

---

104 https://www.pwc.com/gx/en/entertainment-media/outlook-2021/perspectives-2021-2025.pdf

105 https://www.mckinsey.com/business-functions/mckinsey-digital/our-insights/ecosystem-2-point-0-climbing-to-the-next-level

106 https://www.marketplace.org/shows/marketplace-tech/the-gaming-industry-sees-major-revenue-in-going-mobile/

The McKinsey report[107] on Microsoft strategy clearly points out how big technology houses are investing in the fast-growing and revenue-rich gaming industry. This report and the interview with Sarah Bond[108], head of Microsoft's new Gaming Ecosystem Organization, emphasizes the shift from a console-centric approach toward a "ubiquitous global gaming ecosystem" focused not just on gamers but on game developers and publishers. Investments in cloud gaming, the Game Pass subscription service, and cross-platform play have enabled this ecosystem to develop with an eye toward helping gamers participate anywhere, anytime, on any device. It's noteworthy that Xbox Live already has 100 million users and 25 million Game Pass users. Additionally, the premium content for what Microsoft calls the "Netflix of Gaming" currently consists of about 400 million active users in about 200 countries. Obviously, this could lead to the creation of new revenue streams from in-app game purchases and from emerging metaverse plays.

Video game and e-sports revenues are expected to enjoy a 5.7 percent CAGR and become a nearly $200 billion[109] business by year 2027. Other research indicates that the online games market is expected to grow at a CAGR of 9 percent in the forecast period of 2022–2027 to attain a value of $278 billion by 2026[110].

Games as Products

There are different types of associated gaming products, such as gaming consoles, video games that can be downloaded, and games on video (video recordings and live broadcast of games on the ground). All these saleable assets are made available live or offline via marketplaces. Some of these can be sold exclusively, while others, such as "games on video" are often pay-per-view, pay-per-session, or pay-per-season kinds of transactions. As of today, TV sports channels like ESPN[111] dominate the live and recorded game business; however, it will not be long until these games and gaming segments will be made available via other modes of monetization, such as training, crowd entertainment, and sports-data analytics.

107 https://www.mckinsey.com/industries/technology-media-and-telecommunications/our-insights/game-on-an-interview-with-microsofts-head-of-gaming-ecosystem

108 https://www.mckinsey.com/industries/technology-media-and-telecommunications/our-insights/game-on-an-interview-with-microsofts-head-of-gaming-ecosystem

109 https://www.pwc.com/gx/en/entertainment-media/outlook-2021/perspectives-2021-2025.pdf

110 https://www.expertmarketresearch.com/reports/digital-games-market

111 https://www.espn.com/

The major players in the industry are Behaviour Interactive Inc., Sony Corporation, GungHo Online Entertainment America, Inc., Microsoft Corporation, Tencent Holdings Ltd., The Walt Disney Company, Nexon Co., Ltd, and Sega Corporation, among others.

Gaming Platforms or Games as a Service

Gaming platforms basically offer games (mostly, online multi-player games) as a service in which players can sign in and play any chosen games with or without other players. The monetization models can be pay per game, pay an hourly or monthly subscription, or pay a membership fee with unlimited access.

A digital PC game is a program designed to provide an interactive experience to the player. The digital PC games provide a virtual environment with integrated features, such as voice recognition, 3D gaming, GPS tracking, and others in order to provide players with real-life experiences. The game subscription models include both premium and freemium, which are used by social gamers, serious gamers, and core gamers.

Jobs

Job opportunities are a major "entities" commodity that is cataloged and marketed online. One major difference from other commodities is that jobs are not a "saleable" item in the true sense. It's mostly matchmaking; however, there are providers (recruiters or employers), potential consumers (employees), and two kinds of transactions happening. Employers optionally pay the platform owner a fee, often related to the compensation of the recruit. There are other transactional differences— for example, instead of order and receipt, here the offer letter and acceptance become the contractual documents.

The consumer and supplier roles can also be flipped in another marketplace model where the job seekers advertise their availability with published rates of compensation, and the consumers in this case are the employers or hiring people. TaskRabbit and LinkedIn offer such services where the marketplace platform serves the role of connecting the job seekers and job providers.

The Market for Job Platforms

Several billions of dollars are spent on job advertising (Indeed, Glassdoor, LinkedIn, CareerBuilder, and others compete for this market), and even after people apply for ob positions, companies on average spend approximately $4,000 per candidate on nterviewing, scheduling, and assessment to decide if someone is right for a job[112].

Approximately 50 million people in the U.S. change jobs every year. While some of hem are connected directly with their future employer, a large percentage depend on ob marketplaces like Indeed, Glassdoor, LinkedIn, or other online recruiting portals. This evidently shows the large number of stakeholders in this market—employers and employees who are dependent on the job-aggregating platforms.

Forbes[113] projects that the whole job recruitment spend is about $200 billion and that job marketplace platforms will carry 20 to 30 percent of this potential industry expenditure as their potential revenue.

Features of Job Marketplaces

The primary function of a job marketplace is to connect the employers who are seeking candidates with job seekers who are looking for the right job. The process of looking for a match can be initiated by either party. Employers may want to post their job openings and requirements for the candidates. Alternatively, they may want to search for candidates who have already posted their resumes on the marketplace platform. At the same time, candidates—with or without posting their resumes—may be either looking for a specific position of interest or exploring better available opportunities. They also may want to be notified if any potentially interesting openings are advertised.

Given the above scenarios, functions to post openings and resumes and initiate searches for candidates and openings are the primary requirements for any job marketplaces. Grouping or classifying the openings, short-listing candidates, matching the openings based on candidate profile, and sending alerts are some basic features of such marketplaces. Major platforms support more-sophisticated functions, such as resume preparation help, career guidance, salary surveys, facilities at which to conduct job interviews, and collecting and publishing employer ratings.

Job Marketplace Players

There are many job marketplace platforms, both old and new, and some have become dominant.

---

112 https://www.forbes.com/sites/joshbersin/2017/05/26/google-for-jobs-potential-to-disrupt-the-200-billion-recruiting-industry/
113 https://www.forbes.com/sites/joshbersin/2017/05/26/google-for-jobs-potential-to-disrupt-the-200-billion-recruiting-industry/

ZipRecruiter

ZipRecruiter[114] claims that about 110 million users have accessed their services. Powered by AI-matching technology, the platform offers easy and quick search facilities. The company's annual revenue exceeds $700 million. The newly introduced "Act Fast!" label notifies employers if candidates are being actively recruited by other employers and encourages them to reach out quickly.

Indeed

A detailed profile of Indeed was covered in an earlier section.

Upwork

Upwork[115] is a freelance jobs marketplace. Upwork enables clients to interview, hire, and work with freelancers and freelance agencies via the company's platform. Potential clients post a description of their job and a price range they are willing to pay for a freelancer to complete it. Clients may either invite specific freelancers to apply for their jobs or post the job for any freelancer who is interested in applying. Once the client has chosen who they want to complete the job, they hire that freelancer by sending a contract with set hours, pay rate, and a deadline for work completion.

The Upwork platform includes a real-time chat feature that clients and freelancers can use to message prospects. Upwork's time-tracker application records the freelancer's keystrokes and mouse movements and takes screenshots to be submitted to their client. Upwork recorded revenues of $503 million in 2021 with about 150,000 active clients.

Glassdoor

Glassdoor[116] is a portal via which current and former employees can anonymously review companies. The platform also enables users to anonymously submit and view salaries as well as search and apply for jobs. Glassdoor has millions of personalized jobs, salary information, company reviews, and interview questions—all posted anonymously by employees and job seekers. This company's business model includes a marketplace for human resources. It's reported that Glassdoor generates revenue via job listings, job advertising based on the number of advertised postings, employer

---

114 https://www.ziprecruiter.com/
115 https://www.upwork.com/
116 https://www.glassdoor.com

branding, and Glassdoor Review Intelligence, the brand's sentiment analysis platform. In 2019, Glassdoor was acquired for $1.2 billion by Japan's Recruit Holdings.

Monster

Monster[117] is one of the most well-known names in the world of employment websites, with millions of listings on the site at any one time. It's a platform aimed at recruiters, agencies, and employers that handles postings from entry-level and part-time positions to high-level corporate jobs.

Job seekers can sign up for email alerts and use the site's salary comparison tool. The site has a career advice hub with helpful articles about all sorts of employment issues. Users can upload resumes and browse the site's millions of job listings using a range of filtering options.

The site's app also features personalized job recommendations and job quizzes, as well as resume and cover-letter-writing services[118]. The company's revenue stream is based on services like resume preparation, cover letter preparation, advertisements, and tools offered for recruiters.

CareerBuilder

CareerBuilder[119] is an employment website founded in 1995 that operates sites worldwide in more than 60 industry markets. CareerBuilder provides labor market information, talent management software, and other recruitment-related services. It has a powerful job search engine and operates numerous overseas subsidiaries, such as Kariera.gr in Greece; CAO-emplois.com, Erecrut.com, Ingenieur-Emplois.com, LesJeudis.com, Phonemploi.com, and Recrulex.com in France; economicmodeling. com, oilandgasjobsearch.com, Jobmedic.co.uk, and Toplanguagejobs.com in the United Kingdom; and Textkernel in the Netherlands. It also operates niche job search sites, including Sologig.com, Headhunter.com, CareerRookie.com, MiracleWorkers.com, WorkinRetail.com, and JobsInMotion.com.

Social Business and Personal Communication

Social business and personal communication platforms have essentially become powerful ways to generate, share, disseminate, and monetize jobsite contents. Although these contents are not directly monetizable, the sheer traffic and readership

---

117 https://www.monster.com
118 https://www.techradar.com/reviews/monster
119 https://www.careerbuilder.com/

of jobsites lead to tremendous opportunities for commercial advantage via ads, side sales, marketing campaigns, reviews, and their ability to obtain valuable customer preferences and sentiments. Some of the social platforms additionally offer "open marketplaces," such as Facebook Marketplace[120]. The social communication aspect not only benefits consumers, but also provides a strong enterprise presence for marketing, product promotion, training, and brand development. Some sites also offer related services at a cost—for example LinkedIn provides recruitment and online conferences. Further, some sites offer premium memberships with a membership fee. For example, LinkedIn Premium subscriptions at different levels offer new features like private browsing, direct messaging. information on who viewed Your Profile, automatic candidate tracking, lead recommendations, and unlimited access to LinkedIn Learning.

One might think that some of the above-mentioned groups are different from trading marketplaces. However, there are lots of similarities in purpose, function, and site look-and-feel. Whether a site "trades" in connecting people or exchanging commodities, it should facilitate ease of discovery when users are searching for people, so a powerful search engine is a critical common feature. One striking difference between job sites and strictly social ones is that on most social platforms, there are no categorizations, which are conspicuously avoided to rule out any appearance of bias. However, there is support to show the "trending" classifications based on popularity and frequency of search. Another striking difference is the types of contents that are being "marketed". On social platforms, the contents are varied—for example, profiles, opinions, photos, videos, blogs, likes, and comments. There are different ways in which these features are promoted or made prominent on the platform. Providing easy means of onboarding and making updates, posts, downloads, and other basic user functions can be more challenging than providing the functions of traditional commercial marketplaces. Ultimately, it's some form of information—facts, images, status, opinions, and emotions—that is getting "cataloged" and "consumed" on these platforms. Based on the type of social media theme each site is practicing, there are varied ways in which information dissemination happens. Making these features easy to use and providing support and integration with various types of platforms (like mobile and smart devices along with traditional computers) become paramount.

This book isn't intended to cover all the ways in which the various social platforms work; rather, the reason to mention them here is to explain the business model and the marketplace angle of which purveyors of this type of platform t must be cognizant. Also, proprietors of such sites must remain aware of the complex technological

120 https://www.facebook.com/marketplace/learn-more/

challenges related to privacy, security, ethics, bias, and cultural aspects, which are of interest to all platform players.

Social Communication/Sharing Platform

There are hundreds of social business platforms, both small and large. A listing of all of them would soon be out of date as the environment is so dynamic. However, some of the most prominent platform examples include LinkedIn, Meta/Facebook, Twitter, and Instagram. The reason to include them as part of a marketplace discussion is that they do market social interactions indirectly with crowd-sourced producers and consumers. They also have some common functions with traditional e-commerce portals, such as catalog, search, onboarding, memberships, and revenue via premium services and ads. There are other obvious common assets, such as large sets of customer information that the sites can exploit via other commercial channels for product promotions and marketing.

Meetup Platforms

Eventbrite

Eventbrite[121] is an independent platform that lets the users host local events. Members can even send out invitations to potential attendees and let them join the event quickly. Users can also use the platform to sell tickets, which is essential when the event is being used to raise funds for a cause. The site also supports sharing and marketing events. The platform enables an easy way of finding events that match users' preferences. Users may create new events, host events, join an existing event, and sell tickets. As of today, Eventbrite is free to use for free events. Professional membership enables users to sell tickets through the platform and charge a percentage to cater to the event.

Meetup

Meetup[122] is an online service used to create groups that host local in-person and virtual events. Each user can be a member of multiple groups or RSVP for any number of events. Users employ the website to find friends, share a hobby, or conduct professional networking.

Meetup users self-organize into groups. As of 2017, there were more than 200,000 Meetup groups in 180 countries. Each group has a different topic, size, and rules.

121 https://www.eventbrite.com/
122 https://www.meetup.com/

Groups are associated with one of 30+ categories and any number of more than 18,000 tags that identify the group's theme.

Meetup groups are moderated by several organizers. Any Meetup user can be an organizer. Organizers set up groups, organize events, and develop event content. They also pay a fee to run the group, with the expectation that members attending events will eventually share the costs.

OpenSports

OpenSports[123] is a popular sports-management platform. It features leagues, tournaments, pickup games, classes, and memberships. It serves as a place to form a sports group and has features that make managing groups and events easier. It also offers discounted tickets, sports-related chats, and communications. The revenue model includes a monthly membership fee.

Special Interest Groups

While LinkedIn is a generic network used by all types of professionals and nonprofessionals for primarily career and job-related matters, there are several technical and nontechnical groups that specialize on a focus topic. Such communities exist in various areas as diverse as religion, politics, science, marketing, finance, home schooling, photography, gardening, music, or specific games like football, baseball, and cricket. Most of these communities are self-managed and hosted on some standard platforms. The objective of such community platforms is to share information, collaborate among the members, and maybe support or promote common interests of the community. WhatsApp, Google Groups, and Microsoft Teams are good examples in which mostly free platforms exist with some standard functionalities. The platforms often provide basic functions to create groups, add or delete members, share messages and documents, and support different ways of notifying the members.

Discussion Forums

While discussions are part of many social media platforms, discussion forums offer temporary platforms to discuss matters of current interest. Discussion forums[124] are platforms that provide an environment in which participants can pose issues for discussion and respond to any contribution. This creates threaded discussions that can spawn a discussion tree in which the discussions can branch out in many directions

123 https://opensports.net/
124 https://www.gartner.com/en/information-technology/glossary/discussion-forum

(aka subthreads). They are sometimes referred to as "message boards." Multiple online discussion forums exist today. Some prominent ones are Reddit, Quora, GitHub, and Stack Overflow.

Reddit is an online forum that aggregates news from around the world and creates space for online forum users to hold topical discussions and rate web content.

Quora is an online forum that is based on questions and answers regarding various topics and subjects from online forum users around the globe. It has more than 300 million active users every month, and its popularity is still growing.

GitHub is an online forum used globally to converse on topics of common interest among the participants. It also serves as a code repository host for members' content. Members can share their projects because the platform supports different types of files. GitHub developers can also collaborate on or centralize projects.

Stack Overflow is a global online forum that centers on aggregating questions and answers for professional and enthusiast programmers.

Photos, Images, Illustrations

Cheap but high-quality cameras and widespread availability of editing tools have made it easy for nonprofessional users to take quality pictures. This is a crowd-supplied market in which amateur and professional artists create high-quality photos, images, stock videos, illustrations, fonts, and templates. These products are monetized via open marketplaces that offer them to marketers, TV and film producers, media and publishing companies, businesses, and individual creators. Marketers and film and TV producers were the highest revenue generators, holding around 60 percent of the stock videos and stock images market share in 2021[125].

Stock photographs refer to digital images with visual content including people, events, concepts, nature, and objects.

Digital images are helpful for use cases like news stories, blogs, and websites seeking to provide materials for ads or promotional materials. Think of stock photography as the opposite of custom-made photographs, which are licensed directly to a client (depending on copyright status) and are original works created specifically for that client's purpose.

The obvious reason people and organizations purchase digital images is because it's cheaper to buy and download an image from many choices than to hire a photographer. These products are generally sold via a platform that specializes in keeping a large

125 https://shotkit.com/making-money-with-stock-photography/

library of such images so that buyers have multiple options from which to choose. The two most common are macrostock and microstock.

Macrostock photography, also known as "traditional stock photography," refers to agencies that sell high-priced and exclusive images. These agencies license individual images directly to the client and sell the images for between $30 and $3,000. The photographer then gets royalties. The most well-known macrostock agency now is Getty Images, but any company that sells "rights managed" images would qualify.

Microstock agencies, on the other hand, sell images for much less than $10 or on a royalty-free basis. The photographers get no royalties but instead get paid per image download, usually at the end of each month. Companies such as Shutterstock, iStock, Depositphotos, and Dreamstime are all well-established microstock agencies.

Major agencies, such as Getty Images, often additionally represent smaller ones, benefiting from the smaller companies' exclusive content and giving them an additional outlet. Several platforms that cater to amateurs have also started up. The four major vendors that dominate the market are Getty Images, Visual China Group, Shutterstock, and Adobe Stock.

The stock videos and images market is highly competitive, with significant players vying for higher market shares. Intense competition, rapid advances in technology, and frequent changes in end-user preferences constitute significant risks for vendors in this market. These agencies offer all-you-can-eat subscriptions to drive volume and, consequently, revenue growth.

Other prominent vendors in the market are:

- 123RF
- Agence France-Presse
- Agefotostock
- Alamy
- AP Images
- Artlist
- Can Stock Photo
- Coinaphoto

The global market for stock photos and videos is expected to reach $7 billion by 2027 from a current $5 billion[126]. The market for still images has grown 5 percent each year, with 75 percent of all images being sold for commercial purposes, such as

126 https://www.stockphotosecrets.com/stock-agency-insights/stock-photo-market.html

marketing, advertising, and social media usage. Furthermore, the trend of embedding images in audiovisual or interactive productions keeps fueling the demand for stock images today.

Between macrostock and microstock agencies combined, there is an archive of an estimated more than 350 million stock images available online today.

The global stock images and videos market can be divided into different segments based on the targeted end users, which includes marketers and film and TV producers, as well as businesses and individual creators in media and publishing. Marketers and film and TV producers were the highest revenue generators, holding an estimated market share for stock videos and stock images of around 60 percent in 2021.

Below are details of some major stock photo marketplaces.

Adobe Stock

Adobe Stock[127] (formerly Fotolia) was probably the earliest marketplace for photos. They catalog millions of assets—videos, images, photos, music tracks—and have high-quality photos, videos, or vector content. The asset producers own all the rights. Customers can sign up to become an Adobe Stock artist with their Adobe ID and start uploading.

With various subscription plans that include monthly and annual options, members can get high-quality, royalty-free stock photos based on their plan. Also, Adobe offers a kind of "playground" or "development platform" for images and videos as part of its platform. Providers who join Adobe's creator community can sell original photographs, video clips, vectors, and illustrations online.

It's worth noting that a significant percentage of the world's creative professionals use Adobe Photoshop. Adobe's online creative community, Behance, has millions of members worldwide.

Adobe Scan is the leading scanning app on iOS and Android with more than 138 million downloads and two billion documents. Adobe Stock has a stock photo service that is fully integrated into its Creative Cloud platform. It provides a seamless workflow for designers, in which they can browse, test edit, and use professional stock photos in designs or directly in their favorite editing apps.

Creative Cloud provides a solution for professional users who want to create graphics, edit images or videos, animate content, manage large numbers of files, open PDF documents, and handle electronic document signatures, among many other important tasks.

127 https://stock.adobe.com/

Alamy

Alamy[128] is an online supplier of stock images, videos, and other image material. Alamy was founded in 1999 and is headquartered in the United Kingdom. It offers more than 250 million photos and images, to which the company adds more than 100,000 new images every day, sourced from photographers and photo agencies in 173 countries.

Shutterstock

Shutterstock[129] is one of the largest suppliers of stock photography, stock music, and image-editing tools. Shutterstock maintains a library of around 200 million royalty-free stock photos, vector graphics, and illustrations, with around 10 million video clips and music tracks available for licensing. The platform has different business models, such as monthly subscription and other a la carte pricing that includes buying images on demand. Their image-pack deal essentially buys a certain number of downloads and then lets users select images they want from that collection.

Shutterstock has also launched an experiential platform called Shutterstock Labs, an environment for using exploratory tools and products for image search, discovery, and analytics. The company has also launched several iOS and Android apps for contributors. Shutterstock's portal offers more than 400 million images. The company's 2021 reported revenue was about $770 million.

Getty Images

Getty Images[130] was founded in 1995 and has an annual revenue of about $1 billion. Getty Images provides stock photos and imagery collections for advertising and graphic design, as well as print and online publishing. The collection includes diverse imagery for news, sports, entertainment, and archival uses, as well as photo assignment, research, clearance, and licensing services. The company also provides a range of solutions, including Getty Images API, Media Manager, and Studio. Getty Images offers its products for newspapers, magazines, bloggers, and online and broadcast media. Getty Images recently launched VisualGPS Insights[131], a new interactive tool designed to help businesses develop content strategies backed up with data and visual guidance.

128 https://www.alamy.com
129 https://www.shutterstock.com/about
130 https://www.gettyimages.com/
131 https://www.gettyimages.com/visual-gps/insights

Non-Fungible Tokens (NFTs)

An NFT[132] is a digital asset that represents real-world objects like art, music, in-game items, and videos. They are bought and sold online, frequently with cryptocurrency, and they are generally encoded with the same underlying software as many cryptos. An NFT is essentially a line of blockchain code that represents a one-of-a-kind object. NFTs are unique and not mutually interchangeable, which means no two NFTs are the same.

Whether they are gaming cards, rare coins, or a limited-edition pair of Jordans, NFTs create scarcity among otherwise infinitely available assets, and each has a certificate of authenticity to prove it. NFTs are typically used to buy and sell digital artwork and can take the form of GIFs, tweets, virtual trading cards, images of physical objects, video game skins, virtual real estate, and more.

NFTs can be of many different categories—in fact, they can be anything that can be digitized: sports memorabilia, music, pictures, coins, art, games, signatures, celebrity items, antiques, or collectibles. Their value depends on buyer demand.

Emerging NFT Market

NFT sales volume surged past the $25 billion mark in 2021[133]. An NFT can sell for thousands or even millions of dollars. The average price of an NFT rose significantly as interest in NFTs exploded.

NFT Marketplaces

There are many NFT marketplaces for collectibles, art, avatars, and crypto. The field is quickly emerging and yet to mature from its initial craziness.

OpenSea

OpenSea[134] offers a marketplace that enables direct sale of NFTs at a fixed price or via an auction. There are more than 40 million NFTs in OpenSea's catalog. DappRadar reported that a record-breaking 2.4 million NFTs were exchanged on OpenSea in January 2022.

---

132 https://www.forbes.com/advisor/investing/cryptocurrency/nft-non-fungible-token/

133 https://www.fool.com/the-ascent/research/nft-market/

134 https://opensea.io/

The Novatar

The Novatar[135] sells a limited set of 25,000 aging NFT avatars, each with distinct features. Novatar offers NFTs that resemble living beings and are characterized by concepts normally applied to living beings, such as "growing." Each Novatar NFT has a large number of "genes" that makes them characteristically unique over a period (termed "aging").

Crypto.com

Crypto.com NFT[136] is a highly curated NFT marketplace where users can discover exclusive digital collectibles and corresponding NFTs.

Courseware, Knowledge Repositories, Templates

Education is one of the oldest and most fundamental industries. The digitization and internet-centric forms of remote education have triggered courseware and other educational materials to be available for consumers either as freeware or for payment. The recent pandemic and lockdowns all over the globe made education go more remote and digital.

Educational materials form an important class of KIAs. They can be grouped into categories based on the type of education and the types of consumption purposes. Two broad groupings in this area are educational services and educational materials.

Educational services offer the delivery and management of courses, training, badging, or certification. Most online schools provide service offerings like K-12 classes, college and university degree programs, vocational education services, and business in-house training classes on specific topics. Online workshops, paid streaming podcasts, and even yoga, personal physical training, language training, and cooking classes also fall into this category.

While the educational services by themselves have their own assets, educational materials are a voluminous set of assets that are used either as part of educational services or independent of those services, any of which are available for public and paid consumption. These include canned courses, textbooks, lesson plans, guides, quizzes, sample question papers, demos, lectures, diagrams, digital labs, FAQs, and similar materials that are available in different digital formats, including text, graphics, audio, and video. From a marketplace perspective, this category is particularly relevant because it's closest in form to traditional marketplace exchanges.

135 https://thenovatar.com/
136 https://crypto.com/nft/marketplace

Training as a Business

Training and training materials are a huge sector of business in themselves. Aspects of this sector range from tutoring apps, coaching classes, and specialized education packages to providing platforms with which to create educational materials.

The EdTech market size (including hardware) is more than $100 billion as of 2021, with an anticipated CAGR of 20 percent[137]. This may have grown further because of online education expansion during the pandemic.

Some of the prominent players in the global education technology market include the following.

BYJU'S

BYJU'S[138] is an education tutoring app company that runs on a freemium model. It was launched in August 2015, offering educational content for students from grades 4 to 12, and in 2019 the company started an early-learning program for grades 1 to 3. It also trains students for examinations in India, such as IIT-JEE, NEET, CAT, IAS, and international examinations, such as GRE and GMAT.

Academic subjects and concepts are explained using up to 20-minute digital animation videos, via which students learn at a self-paced mode. BYJU'S reports having a 40 million user base and three million annual paid subscribers. Reported revenue is about $300 million and growing.

Anthology

Anthology[139] offers the largest EdTech (educational technology) ecosystem on a global scale for education, recently combining with Blackboard to support more than 150 million users in 80 countries. With a mission to provide dynamic, data-informed experiences to the global education community, Anthology helps learners, leaders, and educators achieve their goals via more than 60 SaaS products and services designed to advance learning.

Teachers Pay Teachers

Teachers Pay Teachers (TpT) is an online marketplace where teachers buy and sell original educational materials. TpT[140] empowers teachers with a catalog of more

137 https://www.grandviewresearch.com/industry-analysis/education-technology-market
138 https://byjus.com/us/
139 www.anthology.com
140 https://www.teacherspayteachers.com/

than five million pieces of educator-created content. The company claims to have a community of more than seven million educators.

Udemy

Udemy, Inc. is an education technology company that provides an online learning and teaching platform. As of June 2023, the platform has 64 million learners, over 20,000 courses, and more than 75,000 instructors teaching courses in nearly 75 languages, with over 870 million course enrollments[141]. Courses are offered in several different areas, such as job-related skills, technical certification, corporate training covering topics like business and entrepreneurship, academics, arts, health and fitness, language, music, and technology.

Udemy also solicits and enables instructors to build online courses on their preferred topics and provides course development tools to instructors to upload videos, PowerPoint presentations, PDFs, audio, ZIP files and any other educational materials for their students. Instructors have the option to interact with users too via online discussion boards. Courses on Udemy can be paid or free, depending on the instructor.

The business model includes custom learning portals by subscription by businesses for in-house training of their employees and organizational licenses for business houses.

Chegg

Chegg[142] provides digital and physical textbook rentals, textbooks, online tutoring, and other student services. Chegg helps users prepare with personalized study recommendations, practice exams, and expert support.

Coursera

Coursera[143] is a massive, open, online course provider founded in 2012 by Stanford University computer science professors Andrew Ng and Daphne Koller. Coursera works with universities and other organizations to offer online courses, certifications, and degrees in a variety of subjects. In 2021, an estimated 150 universities offered more than 4,000 courses through Coursera. Coursera courses last approximately four to twelve weeks, with one to two hours of video lectures a week. These courses provide quizzes, weekly exercises, peer-graded and -reviewed assignments, an optional honors assignment, and sometimes a final project or exam to complete the course. Courses

141 https://about.udemy.com/
142 https://www.chegg.com/
143 https://www.coursera.org

are also provided on-demand with all the course material available at once, which lets users self-pace their learning speed.

EDX

EDX[144] is a massive, open, online course provider created by Harvard and MIT. It hosts online university-level courses in a wide range of disciplines to a worldwide student body, some at no charge. It also conducts research into learning based on how people use its platform. EDX has more than 40 million users and offers more than 3,500 courses.

Udacity

Udacity[145] partners with universities to offer online nanodegree courses, university credit courses, and industry-specific, short-term online courses. Udacity is an online learning platform for those interested in tech-related subjects such as data analysis, software engineering, AI, and web development. Udacity claims more than two million students. Udacity offers 59 nanodegree programs, two executive programs, and 187 free courses. Courses are interactive and visual, and include quizzes, short videos, and projects that students can add to their portfolios. Each course includes several units consisting of video lectures with closed captioning in conjunction with integrated quizzes to help students understand concepts and reinforce ideas, as well as follow-up homework, which promotes a "learn by doing" model.

How Training Gets Productized

Individual course modules on specialty topics are now increasingly being packaged as a "product" to which consumers can subscribe. This type of training started with major technical conferences at which attendees could participate in specific training sessions or workshops. This type of training also includes short-term, nondegree courses offered by traditional schools and universities as continuing education or executive training; however, these were mostly schedule-centric and delivered in person. The evolution of this trend resulted in an explosion of online digital courseware offered as a product. Such courseware suppliers don't offer the material delivery or consumption methods, nor do they enforce any prerequisites. These are self-contained and self-paced course modules that don't offer any certification or validation of the skill or knowledge acquired. There's no set syllabus, nor are there prescribed textbooks. The courseware is packaged with reading materials, lectures, videos, exercises, and sometimes self-testing sessions.

144 https://www.edX.com/
145 https://www.udacity.com/

In the beginning, such courseware was offered by well-established organizations like Coursera or Udemy, and the courseware was produced and owned by the same organization. Eventually, some of these organizations started cataloging third-party course packages as well. Now, authors can publish and monetize their courseware through the education marketplaces. These marketplaces provide infrastructure and tools to build an online course easily and quickly so that the authors can focus on the content. Creators bring their own curriculum and content and pay different levels of fixed monthly subscription fees for powerful platforms. Distribution, however, is the creators' sole responsibility.

In addition, these platforms help to publish, advertise, and sell these courses to the captive users the platforms already have. Beyond education, online marketplaces connect buyers and sellers (in this case, learners and trainers or teachers) on a proprietary platform. The marketplace doesn't hold any type of inventory itself but instead helps the buyers and sellers facilitate a transaction. Sellers can focus on their core competency, thereby providing customers with the most relevant products. Such platforms help learners everywhere acquire knowledge and skills.

There are several players in this field. Some major ones are Udemy, Khan Academy, and Coursera.

Skillshare[146] is a platform providing resources for teaching creative skills. One can find courses on all kinds of topics, both popular and niche, including such varied topics as marketing, photography, cooking, hand painting, doodling, and even wall hanging.

Coaching and Tutoring

Online coaching or tutoring offerings target specific short-term purposes like SAT coaching, language tutoring, and yoga classes. These are characterized by well-curated specialty programs with multiple sessions frequently created and offered by the online platform owners themselves.

The Economy of Educational Materials and Services

The global education technology market size was valued at $106.46 billion in 2021 and is expected to expand to $500 billion[147] by 2030. Education technology (Ed Tech) includes hardware and software technology used to educate students via virtual methods to improve learning in classrooms and enhance students' education outcomes. Udemy had an approximate revenue of $500 million in 2021.

146 https://www.skillshare.com/
147 https://www.grandviewresearch.com/industry-analysis/education-technology-market

Digital Ads and Promotions

Within the advertising business, there are two major parts of each commercial transaction. One is the ad itself, which is often customized, but many ad agencies have styles, formats, shells, and stock videos available from which customers can select for different products.The second part is the actual ad spots appearing on various mass and online media platforms. The nature of business varies widely, based on the media on which an ad appears. Currently, these transactions are accomplished via B2B direct deals, with ad agencies often simply being intermediaries.

There can be differences of opinion as to whether advertising is a service or a commodity. Advertising can be a commodity if the potential advertiser is buying advertising on a TV station, simply because of television's mass reach. Some people consider ads to be part of a plan or strategy that an advertiser is carrying out, categorizing those as a resource rather than a commodity. Advocates of this definition cite the example of buying advertising during a specific television program that reaches the targeted market with an ad that includes a tailored message. This controversy shows there can be a thin line between considering advertising a commodity or a resource, depending on how generic an ad's content, format, and media slot are.

An online article from IAB[148] discusses how the commodity-vs.-resource confusion is caused by the effort of many large ad agency media-buying groups to disenfranchise branded publishers by launching their own "demand-side platforms"—essentially, stock exchanges for the trading of online advertising inventory—for the purpose of driving the marginal cost of production and distribution of billions of commodity products called banners, spots, and pages to as close to zero as it can be. Some concepts associated with demand-side platforming are online networks, demand-side exchanges, and real-time bidding, as well as inventory, buying agencies, and procurement offices. Several such demand-side platforms have sprung up—for example, Smaato[149], and InMobi[150]. Smaato's Digital Ad Tech Platform offers a free ad server and monetization solution that connects quality publishers with premium marketers to engage audiences around the world. The platform's traffic volume, astonishingly, already tops billions.

Ad-trading platforms provide data that helps agencies optimize advertising for their clients. The potential data covers everything from providing insights on consumer behavior to finding ad placements that generate more demonstrable returns.

---

148 https://www.iab.com/news/is-marketing-a-strategic-resource-or-a-procured-commodity/

149 https://www.smaato.com/

150 https://www.inmobi.com/exchange

Ecosystem Playgrounds for KIAs

"Playground" is a general term that represents a place or platform for practicing, experimenting, testing, and developing new products, experiences, or applications.

"Ecosystem playground" is a general reference for an environment for content development, testing, and experimentation. Both consumers and providers can use the tools and resources provided on such platforms to share and gain familiarity with the tools and use them to prototype and simulate potential content as a community.

The playgrounds are essential components of any marketplace of KIA products, such as software, data, models, APIs, and similar items.

Depending on the area and asset characteristics, the facilities and functions of the playground may differ. The following sections describe playgrounds in different types of marketplaces.

Developers' Playgrounds

A developer typically needs quick access to the tools, training, and documentation to build an intended application. A user-friendly development environment that offers APIs, libraries, databases, external interface apps—as well as tools with which to compile, build, and test the application—can be invaluable. These developers' playgrounds are typically cloud-based and equipped with test suites, data for testing applications, and deployment facilities. Moreover, as most development occurs in cycles and often involves more than one developer, another essential component is version-management tools. Guided tutorials with which to experience and run sample applications, the ability to publish and promote the application, integration with popular code, and document management apps via GitHub integration to export the code can also be essential to any developers' playground.

There are many platform suppliers in this area, such as IBM Technology Sandbox[151] and IBM API Hub.

Modelers' Playgrounds

A modelers' playground is analogous to a developers' playground; however, it's specific to AI model development. In addition to traditional application development needs, the modelers' playground potentially requires data sets that modelers can use to test and compare model algorithms, a collection of core model APIs that data owners who want to create new data insights can use, as well as tools with which to check the trustworthiness of models, model deployment facilities, and model security

151 https://developer.ibm.com/

applications—all must be at hand. In addition, sample data sets with which to build models will also be an essential component. Tools to generate Synthetic data in a chosen domain to support model building are also helpful. Efforts are underway to build large-scale deep neural network (DNN) models (such as foundation models), which are also potential services or functions that should be part of future modelers' playgrounds.

Several commercial and open-source modelers' playground platforms are already in operation. The LF AI initiative on Machine Learning eXchange (MLX) led by IBM data scientists is one such example.

Virtual Studios

Virtual studio, another variation of the development playground, is meant for virtual construction of physical goods, such as buildings and artworks, as well as entertainment products such music, videos, and games. There are several mobile apps and cloud-based virtual studios available to produce, test, and publish near-professional-quality audio and video productions. Livestream Studio[152] illustrates an example of software and services that enable video productions with professional live streams. Livestream Studio supports the use of multiple camera inputs and includes a customizable graphics library to add dynamism and sophistication to any live event. The mobile app iMovie[153] helps users create movies and trailers from video files. It comes with a pre-installed video editing application developed by Apple for macOS, iOS, and iPadOS devices.

Virtual Theaters and Classrooms

A theater in which producers can organize events isn't a new concept—except if it's a virtual one. As virtual musical programs, movie shows, meetups, conferences, and political campaigns proliferate, there's a need for more sophisticated tools and platforms to support conducting them. Webex, Zoom, and Microsoft Teams are addressing many necessary functions; however, they are all a far cry from real environments. As is typical with any event venues and event management, multiple functional components—such as stages, panels, banners, exhibition booths, breakout rooms, whiteboards, flip charts, and interactive Q&A facilities—are relevant.

With the advent of the metaverse and other digital tools and technologies, sophisticated near real-time immersive virtual classrooms have become another lab or

---

152 https://livestream.com/production
153 https://www.videowinsoft.com/imovie-movie-maker-mac.html

factory with which users can create courseware and supporting educational materials. Such classrooms are expected to provide near-real experiences for teaching and learning on many different topics, be they about science, art, geography, history, or any other topic. The immersive experience that can be facilitated by metaverse technology opens the immense possibility of virtual classrooms, schools, and universities with two major impacts. First is the ability to take quality education to every nook and corner of world (for example, a student doesn't need to be in any particular location to attend high-standard education offered by Stanford, MIT, or Imperial College). Second, the interactive facilities can lead to individualized education and coaching, which is currently severely limited because of lack of resources (e.g., individual expert teachers and their bandwidth).

Virtual Sports and Game Playgrounds

With the proliferation of online games, virtual playgrounds that are probably the most popular are the ones where two or more players can meet and engage in competitive or entertainment-specific games. The platform's responsibility is to provide onboarding of users, cataloging of games, management of the individual sessions (including tracking proficiency levels and scores), and sometimes the tasks of matching players and organizing sessions and seasons for gaming events. Games and sports are among the most popular areas of virtual business, with huge revenue potential. Many gaming platforms have mushroomed, including those from giants like Microsoft, which recently made news through the largest acquisition of a tech company (Activision) so far.

Recap

KIAs are undoubtedly the most valuable products, as well as those best suited, for transactions via online marketplaces. The combined value of different types of KIAs could easily surpass $10 trillion per year soon, which would make them the most business-critical trading commodity across all industry sectors. Trading of KIAs brings in new social, business, and technical challenges, as well as legitimate concerns. However, good engineering of the processes and technology-enabled solutions guided by ethical principles and regulations will open the possibility of monetization and use of KIAs for the benefit of society. The brief review of different types of KIAs in this chapter illustrates the immense scope and diversity of suppliers, consumers, and use cases.

CHAPTER 5

MARKETPLACE FUNCTIONS FOR KIA ASSETS

Introduction

Several functions are standard and essential for running a digital marketplace. These digital versions of any commercial establishment, like their brick-and-mortar counterparts, need the abilities to procure the products, display and price them, manage the sales transactions (including billing and payments), and deliver the goods purchased. Although these may sound simple and obvious, challenges arise when these basic operations need to be scaled up and made global. All these steps should ideally be efficient in aiding growth, profitability, and customer satisfaction. The ways in which a business automates these operations, measures and analyzes operational-health data, and makes data-driven decisions are the key drivers that require closer consideration than traditional basic functions.

Vendor Development

Most critical to the success of any marketplace is the presence of a rich, diverse, and competitive set of products from a multitude of suppliers. One major reason that people shop at Amazon, Walmart[154], Target[155], or eBay is the abundance and variety of goods they can buy at one location. So, the most critical function or capability of any marketplace is the ease and speed with which vendors can be onboarded. This function requires far more than simply registering a vendor at the marketplace. It also involves developing and growing strong relationships with a large set of sellers. This is a

154 www.walmart.com
155 www.target.com

multi-step process, starting with creating a policy compliant with internal and external regulations and laws, prequalifying and vetting the vendors, defining and refining the specifications of the supplies, and negotiating and finalizing prices and long-term seller contracts with scope, terms, and conditions. It continues through setting up vendor accounts to give vendors access to a self-service portal, enabling vendor training, facilitating an attractive incentive scheme, and establishing proper accounting and payment processes. Then there are the matters of collecting vendor transaction data, analyzing and sharing the same to measure and improve vendor performance, establishing a vendor-rating system, and maintaining ongoing communications with vendors.

Considering the complexity of the vendor development process, as in many other cases, automation is the key to success in scaling. For example, Amazon has around 10 million sellers worldwide[156], and it adds about one million new vendors every year[157]. The third-party vendors contribute about 40 percent of Amazon's business, which shows the necessity of supporting fast and friction-free onboarding of vendors to the platform. Such massive scaling may be an exception; however, all marketplaces need to have a clear scheme for building a large and diverse set of vendors to make their product suite rich and attractive.

Display of Products/Catalogs

In both online and brick-and-mortar shops, the organization of the store and the display of the products are critical for customers to easily find the right product and accelerate the purchase process. This involves categorizing and listing products in a meaningful way, providing all necessary details (including price and manufacturers' information), and offering an easy means for purchasing them. The larger the product set, the more challenging the problem. This entails a kind of marketing within the shop itself.

156 https://www.edesk.com/blog/amazon-statistics/
157 https://www.helium10.com/blog/how-many-sellers-on-amazon/

Figure 5.1: Digital Catalogs

In fact, digital catalogs are becoming a must even for brick-and-mortar commercial establishments. A common example is the digital menu, which is a digitized version of a restaurant menu available to customers via QR codes. The advantages are obvious and attractive, such as the ease with which items and prices can be updated and the opportunity to provide a more real-life experience by providing photographs and videos and the ability to rate and rank the items by consumers.

Categories and Hierarchies

Besides the availability of products and prices, the next most important factor for facilitating commercial transactions is the ability to catalog and display marketplace products. Ease of finding a desired item is key to retaining customers and clinching deals. Although this may not be an issue when the number of products is small, ignoring this factor is not realistic for any sizeable marketplace or one planning expansion.

It is worth noting that Amazon has a catalog of 350 million products. Walmart has roughly 25 million items for sale, and eBay has 1.6 billion items listed. These numbers, of course, belong to the largest e-sellers and show how far scaling can go. The critical challenge then is how to organize and display such a large set of items to enable customers with varied interests and preferences to find them. Two major functions necessary to support large selections are a well-organized catalog and a powerful and fast search engine to sort through them. Any search will be aided heavily by the way the catalog is organized.

Categorizing the products into manageable and meaningful buckets and labeling or annotating them correctly are mammoth challenges. The task is compounded if there is a need to add new products frequently—perhaps even every minute of the day. The categories cannot be static. They will evolve, become disrupted, and get reshuffled as products change, new products arrive, and social and business viewpoints change. For example, there was no category called "intelligent agents" for Amazon Echo or Google Assistant until a couple of years ago. The categories in which to place television sets are changing almost every month because of technological advances and the way televisions are constructed. In short, cataloging cannot be done manually. Automated cataloging and crowd-sourced cataloging are the only ways the platforms can keep up with the size, scale, and diversity of products available to sell. The challenges can be summarized as follows.

Size and diversity of products: As a business scales, the types and number of products expand manyfold, and the catalog framework and process need to handle such evolutionary growth dynamics.

Dynamic nature of the product mix: Products get dropped and added based on market demand as well as when the designs and the underlying technology change. Maintaining a catalog in a dynamic fashion poses even larger issues than building one.

Changes of suppliers and vendors: Typical marketplaces support different vendors and suppliers, which means the categorization of products may not all have the same criteria.

Stakeholders with varied interests: User interests are widely different, based on their backgrounds, objectives in looking for products, and current geolocation. This means one way of grouping or displaying may not be appealing to all.

Multi-dimensional categorization: An item can be classified in multiple ways, from as simple as by vendor to tiny feature-specific groupings. For example, a TV can be grouped as LED or LCD (technology-specific), 45-inch or 72-inch (based on size), price point, Samsung or Sony (based on make), or smart or non-smart (based on internet connectivity). While a separate catalog may not be needed for each of these dimensions, a dynamic search and display based on several such features would require a rich set of attributes to help distinguish and categorize easily.

Hierarchical categorization: A hierarchical categorization from major types to subtypes to sub-subtypes is the focus of any classification scenario. This helps provide iterative drill down, easy navigation, and better structuring. Typically, this approach is pplied to well-established domains with widely accepted nomenclatures for groups and subgroups. Good examples will be broad categories like furniture, stationery, apparel, electronics, software, and vegetables. Each of these categories will have subsequent subgroups, such as televisions, computers, mobile phones, and printers under the electronics category.

Catalog Content Structure and Style

It is not enough to only facilitate search and display based on user queries. The items presented need to be well described to provide useful information to the consumers so they can decide whether the product meets their requirements and whether the product qualifies for purchase. This means that the product description should cover information presented in incremental detail. Pictures of the items (if physical) along with functional and technical specifications are essential. Moreover, as in Amazon catalogs, customer reviews and ratings and product comparisons are desirable functions. Videos and 3D simulations also have started appearing, especially when a potential purchase involves items like homes, appliances, or toys. In fact, the "trial versions" of music, games, or software make further advances possible in providing additional user experiences to help the customers reach a "buy" decision.

Dynamic Catalog Displays

One of the big advantages of online marketplaces is that it's much easier to make updates to product displays as compared to doing that in brick-and-mortar shops with physical goods. Moving items onto the shelves and changing their positions are typically laborious tasks. The need for frequent catalog changes arises in many ways. Product portfolios, prices, promotion of products on the landing page and other pages, and the ways in which items are categorized will all change frequently. The classic example is the Amazon e-commerce platform itself. As seasons change and new products arrive, the catalog is updated—sometimes even on an hourly basis. This dynamic catalog stands out in contrast with the old printed catalogs, which were cumbersome to update and distribute. Keeping the catalogs up to date and relevant to the consumers is key to making the sales happen quickly, enabling upselling and cross-selling, or even helping to keep the customers coming back and staying longer.

Dynamic cataloging is possible only with automation tools that examine various data points, such as day of the month, time of day, types of new products, price changes, market pulse, and recent events (e.g., sales-relevant holidays). Intelligent models need to be in place to recommend what to display, where, and with what prominence on the pages. This model also needs to be continually fine-tuned based on transactional patterns, geography, and types of users. (More details on automation needs will be covered in a later chapter.)

Personalized Catalogs

Gone are the days when every customer sees the same catalog in style and contents. Digital catalogs enable rearrangement of products to suit each individual user or type of user. The user profiling and segmentation based on previous purchases, browsing history, and preferences can be effectively used to display the products that interest the user on the landing pages and in subsequent searches.

Personalization of catalogs involves providing a better user experience based on shopping history, personal profile, preferences, and interests. Customizing the product recommendations helps users find the products they are looking for by letting them quickly search relevant new products, deals, and promotions (also known as providing personalized search priority); ranking the results; and enhancing marketing communications by personalizing push notifications and on-page advertisements.

All these functions, no doubt, offer ways to improve sales and upselling or cross-selling opportunities. It's important to note that personalization of catalogs is not a one-time job but needs to continually happen as time passes, seasons change, new products arrive, and price variations take place.

Amazon Personalize[158] is a tool from AWS that helps users create their own personalized catalogs.

Catalog Search and Product Discovery

Searching the catalog is essentially finding the right product on the platform. Searches can be user-initiated by typing in keywords, which is often considered a "pull data" approach. Alternatively, products may be displayed or "pushed" into a customer's attention, based either on sales strategy or customer profile and preferences.

Pricing and Price Policies

The price of a commodity or a charge for a service is probably the most critical factor in any sales transaction. People often overlook quality, long waits, and age of the goods in favor of a competitive price, depending on the situation. On the other hand, price sometimes isn't a consideration when it comes to scarcity and essentiality of goods, urgency of need, or who the buyer is. Also, in a luxury market, the brand, quality, and

158 https://aws.amazon.com/personalize/

the user experience may overtake the price consideration. In summary, right pricing is a critical step and often a complex process influenced by season, type of product, demand, competition, availability, and a host of other market dynamics.

A McKinsey report [159]declares that "pricing is by far the biggest tool for earnings improvement." This makes price a strategic tool without affecting cost optimization or investment tuning. The report states that a 1 percent improvement in pricing raises profits by 6 percent, on average.

The following sections cover different pricing strategies and their impacts on commerce.

Fixed (Flat) Pricing

Some say that the idea of fixed pricing (in which the seller chooses a price that is available to all buyers in the market) was originated by Quaker merchants in Philadelphia[160]. The Quakers, a historically Christian denomination, believed that because everyone is equal before God, everyone should be charged the same price. Charging people different amounts for the same item, just because of their appearance, status, or haggling ability, was considered immoral!

In the 1800s, fixed pricing and price tags became a norm, partly because of the move from mom-and-pop shops to chain department stores. Bargaining and bidding are often considered an inefficient process, especially when the purchasers far outnumber the suppliers.

Tiered Pricing

Tiered pricing is a variation of fixed pricing. Prices are indicated in terms of tiers, enabling the unit cost to change with quantity or usage. The basic idea is to offer lower rates for customers who consume larger quantities. This is a win-win opportunity for both sides because as consumption gets higher, the price gets lower. This would encourage buyers to commit to bulk orders and repeat orders, and high-volume business is obviously attractive to the vendors as well.

Usage-Based Pricing

This model is applicable for services like hourly labor or utility services. It requires a metering scheme to measure the amount of consumption. With the usage-based model,

---

159 https://www.mckinsey.com/business-functions/growth-marketing-and-sales/our-insights/pricing-the-next-frontier-of-value-creation-in-private-equity

160 https://aifora.com/en/blog-en/the-history-of-pricing-from-the-barter-system-to-dynamic-pricing/

customers are charged based on how much they consume in a regular billing cycle. Often, there is no commitment as with flat-rate pricing models, and sometimes the price is collected before the billing cycle. A mixed model of consumption rate plus a minimum fee is also quite popular.

Dynamic Pricing

Dynamic pricing is a strategy in which the prices for a product or service are updated based on current supply and demand. These updates can be seasonal, daily, or even hourly. Flash sales, pre-announced sales, and price adjustments (often downward) are variations of this pricing policy. The objective can be manyfold: increase the volume of sales even at the cost of sacrificing the profit margin a bit, attract buyers to the platform in hopes of getting additional business through sale of other goods, reduce backed-up inventory, and sometimes, just to beat the competition by increasing market share at any cost. It's important to note that dynamic pricing doesn't mean a permanent reduction or increase of prices, but rather changing it slightly to stir up the market.

Dynamic pricing emerged in the 1980s, driven by technological innovations. It was pioneered by the airline industry, which used factors such as departure time, destination, and season to automate the prices for flights. Soon, other verticals in the tourism industry, like hotels and car rentals, followed suit. More recently, retailers have also adopted dynamic pricing, with online giants like Amazon leading the way.

The main idea behind dynamic pricing is that it's flexible and based on real-time data[161]. To effectively implement dynamic pricing, a diverse set of real-time data must be collected and analyzed, and appropriate recommendations based on pricing levels must be generated. The data set may include market demand, inventory, supply chain, competition prices, market sentiment, and other factors. Analysis of this real-time data using optimal pricing models built from historical data requires employing advanced technologies in data science and AI. (More on this will be found in a later chapter.)

Entitled Pricing

An entitled price is a certain price level that's offered from one business to another exclusively for the purchase of an asset. Entitlement offers are nontransferable and valid for an agreed-upon timeframe by the two parties. This pricing model has been adopted by two trusted partners between which there is a long-term business agreement for purchasing goods. Typical examples are preapproved hotel rates, car-rental rates,

---

161 https://www.business.com/articles/what-is-dynamic-pricing-and-how-does-it-affect-ecommerce/

or preferred prices for specific goods that employees can purchase from an approved vendor. The entitled or negotiated price is arrived at by a consumer and vendor anticipating but not guaranteeing a total volume of transactions. Sometimes, the terms and conditions may also include a price variation below or above certain thresholds. This is essentially a convenient contract price between two businesses so that each purchase need not be negotiated. It also ensures that there is uniform pricing for a prescribed period (such as one year) between the vendor and consumer. This pricing model is quite prevalent in B2B transactions, especially for software licenses, hardware leasing, and accessory supplies. The entitled pricing model is also used for equities and employee purchase plans.

Payments

Making payments for purchases is an integral part of all commercial transactions. Unlike in-person purchases, online trades require compatible remote payment schemes. Knowing the forms of payment that the customers prefer to use for online purchases is valuable in setting up marketplaces. Many marketplaces offer multiple forms of payment schemes[162], including those below:

- *Credit Cards:* Credit cards are one of the most popular and straightforward ways to pay both offline and online. Credit card payments are one of the most frequent forms of electronic payments. When a customer uses a credit card to purchase anything, the credit card issuer bank pays on the customer's behalf, and the customer has a specific amount of time to pay the credit card bill.

- *Debit Cards:* A debit card is like a credit card. Customers can enter their bank account details, making this the equivalent of paying in cash or by check. The main difference between a debit card and a credit card is that when using a debit card, the money is immediately deducted from an associated bank account, and there must be enough money in that account to complete the transaction. However, there is no such requirement with a credit card transaction.

- *Digital Wallets:* Digital wallets are a growing online payment method and include PayPal, Venmo, Apple Pay, Google Pay, and Amazon Pay, as well as buy-now-pay-later solutions like Affirm, Afterpay, Klarna, and Sezzle. Digital wallets enable customers to pay by simply logging into their digital wallet service during checkout to authorize the payment. Some people prefer this payment method

162 https://www.frbsf.org/cash/publications/fed-notes/2021/may/2021-findings-from-the-diary-of-consumer-payment-choice/

because they only need to remember their login. According to one recent survey, 75 percent of all consumers now use digital payment schemes[163].

Figure 5.2: Digital Wallets

- *Digital Currency:* Using digital currency, such as Bitcoin or other cryptocurrencies, is still emerging and represents only a small portion of sales use.
- *Buy Now Pay Later (BNPL)* was a substitute for a debit card or cash. "A lower-cost financing option" was the most cited reason for BNPL use.

Some of the most popular and emerging payment services (especially for digital wallets) are:

- *PayPal:* PayPal is one of the most well-known and well-established methods of online money transfer. It is available in a variety of countries and supports more than 25 currencies. It accepts credit cards, provides a digital wallet, and even offers loans. PayPal is built on powerful technology that lets marketplaces easily accept credit and debit cards, offer PayPal to their customers, and extend BNPL options.
- *Amazon Pay:* Amazon Pay is a popular e-commerce gateway for mobile platforms. It enables merchants to process both online and offline payments on their smartphones. The transaction is immediate and can be done without any registration. The e-commerce payment processing uses tap-to-pay technology, a peer-to-peer approach. To use Amazon Pay, users need an Amazon Payments account. The service meets all the requirements of e-commerce merchants, such as providing billing address, business transacted, and its owners' information. Amazon Pay simplifies checkout for hundreds of millions of Amazon customers by enabling them to use payment and shipping information stored in their

163 https://fintechmagazine.com/digital-payments/75-of-consumers-now-using-mobile-wallets-survey

Amazon accounts. According to Amazon, some merchants who use Amazon Pay have experienced increased conversion, reduced cart abandonment, and faster checkouts. Amazon Pay offers fraud-detection technology and Amazon's A-to-Z Guarantee on qualified orders. Moreover, mobile checkout takes just a few taps.

- *Google Pay:* Google Pay is a digital wallet and payment platform. It enables users to pay for transactions with Android devices in-store and on supported websites, mobile apps, and Google services, like the Google Play Store. Users can link credit or debit cards to their Google Pay account, which is used for making the transactions for in-store or online purchases. On Android devices, Google Pay uses near-field communication (NFC) to interact with payment terminals. When signed into one's Google account in the Chrome browser, users can conduct transitions with Google Pay on sites that support the service.

- *Opayo:* Opayo (formerly Sage Pay) is one of the e-commerce payment solutions that helps merchants optimize their checkout process, accelerate online payment processing, and secure payment information carefully. Customers can use any paying card to purchase their items online via Opayo.

- *Stripe:* In addition to offering fast, easy, and secure payment acceptance, Stripe works with Google Pay, Apple Pay, and Masterpass to offer customers even more payment options on carts and checkout pages. Stripe is PCI-certified and accepts international transactions from customers worldwide. Stripe works with some of the country's most well-known B2C, SaaS, and product companies. There are no monthly fees, but processing fees are calculated based on the transaction size. The service can handle high-transaction volumes and provides good integration and support.

- *2Checkout:* 2Checkout is available in a wide range of countries and is one of the most cost-effective payment processors available. It offers both hosted and online shopping carts. However, the API is complicated, making integration with e-commerce platforms difficult.

- *Square:* With Square, users can transact both online and offline (if that is suitable for different kinds of in-person and online purchases). Square enables sales online and in person with two-way inventory sync and provides a robust suite of tools to help cooperating merchants grow their business and improve their operations. Features include payroll and time management, employee-specific access management, customer engagement, and online invoices.

- *Payeezy:* This is one of the oldest payment solutions and has served users since 2008. It provides simplified e-commerce payment solutions to all companies in diverse industries. It accepts various payment methods, such as credit cards, debit cards, gift cards, and other prepaid card offerings.

- *BlueSnap:* BlueSnap is a single global platform that accepts payments from anywhere and on any device, offering global payment processing and multi-currency support. It supports more than 100 currencies and lets shoppers select from 16 payout currencies within a single account. With BlueSnap, merchants can accept major credit card payments, as well as regional cards like China Union Pay.

- *Klarna:* Klarna users can access no-liability financing options at checkout, including built-in fraud protection.

- *Sezzle:* Sezzle enables shoppers to split orders into four interest-free payments over six weeks in more than 44,000 online stores. With no impact on credit scores and by offering free payment reschedules, it's a convenient and easy-to-manage payment option for customers.

Incentives and Royalties

Awarding incentives to stakeholders such as vendors, salespeople, customers, and employees is a common practice in the marketplace world. Devising the incentive plan, publishing it, and managing its implementation are often important factors of business growth. Specific tools and software are employed for effective incentive management. A recent report by the Incentive Federation Inc. (IFI) [164] narrates the current scenario of the company's incentive program for boosting sales. This report reveals that 84 percent of U.S. businesses spend $176 billion annually on award points, gift cards, trips and travel, merchandise, and experiential rewards to inspire sales staff, employees, channel partners, and customers.

The IFI report notes that "incentive spending directed at the following distinct targets" can offer the following benefits:

- Reward and motivate desired behaviors and achievements among a company's salespeople.

- Reward and motivate desired behaviors and achievements among a company's distributors, channel, or dealer partners.

---

164 https://www.incentivefederation.org/wp-content/uploads/2022/08/IFI-2022-Research-Study-Final-Report-1.pdf

- Reward and motivate desired behaviors and achievements among a company's employees.
- Reward and motivate a company's customers as part of a loyalty program.
- Show appreciation to clients, prospective clients, or partners for their business.

Order Management

Transactions don't end with receiving confirmed orders. In some sense, it's only the beginning of another major phase of e-commerce. Order management involves two different groups of functions; one for the consumer, which includes order tracking, order modification, and order cancellation, and one for the marketplace, which includes order execution, delivery, order account management, order analytics, and collection of order feedback. The user-friendly set of order management functions contributes significantly to customer satisfaction. Online order management functions need to be complete and easy to use because customers and vendors rarely meet in person. Order execution is a post-process in online commerce, as opposed to buying an in-stock item from a conventional retail shop via a personal transaction. This means continuous tracking and communication within online customer relationships are an important part of maintaining those relationships.

Order Creation

Customer selection of one or more items and confirmation of the purchase by paying or agreeing to pay the billed amount creates an order. The order-creation function needs to compute individual line-item prices by considering the quantity ordered, calculating any needed price adjustments, computing the total order value, applying sales tax and any other tariffs as applicable, and adding the delivery charges (including any installation or onsite services optionally selected). To complete the order typically requires the addition of customer details and an address to which the items will be delivered. A requested delivery date and a committed delivery date are also part of the order details. Typically, the vendor assigns a unique order number, which becomes the reference for any communications and transactions beyond the point of order placement. Most of the online ordering process involves billing and payment or commitment to pay to secure and confirm the order.

Order Editing and Cancellation

Even "firm" orders may need to be updated or even canceled, which can happen at any time until item delivery. These changes could include increasing or decreasing the quantity of any of the items ordered, replacing or upgrading one or more items (if that is allowed), rescheduling the delivery date(s), and modifying delivery location(s). These operations sometimes may involve a charge and/or may impose certain penalties. depending on the contract and the order's age and status. Typically, the order is "frozen" once the items are delivered, and then it falls into a "return" process, which may have its own rules and procedural steps.

Order Tracking

Order tracking facilitates the ability to check the status of the order, basically the delivery, payment, and any updates. Most online orders may need one or more days for delivery and payment and closure of the order. Tracking the stages of the order is important from a customer perspective, as well as from the internal accounting and reporting perspective. The revenue realization often depends on the specific status of the order. In today's world, continuous communication of the order status is implemented via multiple modes, such as text messages or emails.

Shipping and Delivery

One major advantage of KIA products is that delivery of goods can be electronic. Although this method avoids the delays of shipping (including physical transportation), it doesn't necessarily make delivery easy. The packaging and electronic delivery of many KIA products, their peculiar intricacies given the assets' size, and the real-time nature of the KIA assets (such as streaming videos and data, large images, and models) can complicate the delivery process. The diverse formats and content types often make KIA product delivery challenging.

Three generic approaches to delivery are "push," "pull," and "hosting."

The push strategy transports the assets from the supplier platform to the consumer platform. This is the most common method if the consumers have their own computing or other platform for asset-storage and processing.

In the pull method, the buyer essentially triggers the transportation. The asset owner provides the access privileges and location link to the buyers and then buyers download the assets at their convenience. The main difference is that the buyers control the speed of transfer, time of transfer, formats (from a given set of options) of transfer, and the asset-transfer location.

In the hosting approach, the assets aren't physically transferred; however, the access privileges to own and use them are provided as part of the purchase. Many cloud-based Asset as a Service (AaaS) purchases fall into this category. Sometimes, a copy of the asset is moved to a private cloud space that is owned by the buyer within the asset hosting platform (if that option is supported). Many AWS cloud-based assets work in this fashion. This has many advantages, such as avoiding delays, format mismatches, or asset security concerns during delivery. This method grants instantaneous ownership transfer and enables monitoring by both supplier and consumer. This method also benefits small-scale users who may not have their own appropriate computing and storage resources. In this situation, however, the asset supplier and the marketplace itself need to provide additional storage and computing power to facilitate adequate security and privacy for the buyer's assets. Another advantage of the hosted method is that the bug fixes and updates with newer versions are easier to carry out.

Updates and Upgrades

One of the critical differences between KIA assets and other traditional goods is that KIA assets are often undergoing constant revisions and purchase agreements often include free or nominal access to later upgrades. This means that the delivery of goods isn't on a one-time basis; connections with buyers must be maintained regarding availability and delivery of newer versions of the assets. As mentioned earlier, delivery of upgrades or newer versions is much easier in a hosted environment because no physical transfer of assets is needed.

Continuous Delivery

Some purchased assets are subscribed for a specific period. Such assets may be dynamically changing—for example, streaming sensor data and broadcasts of real-time events like news, concerts, conferences, classes, and games. The delivery of goods doesn't have a fixed duration or end, and this poses several challenges. These include real-time performance via an adequate communication bandwidth, reliable connections, security, privacy that needs to be operational on live data, and live feedback measurements.

Returns

In traditional sales, including online marketplaces, the ability to return the purchased goods is an essential process step. Many customers don't like a "sales are final" policy. Today most brick-and-mortar and online sales happen with the condition that items can be returned within a specified time, although this may not be applicable for perishable goods. Often, the customers need not even specify a reason. This freedom to cancel the order and get their money back is an attractive feature for increasing sales because customers feel there is less risk in buying an item. They can try it, and if it's damaged, it's not usable for whatever reason, or they simply don't like it, they can return it. Some suppliers do charge a nominal restock fee for high-priced items. Some other sales offer only a store credit rather than cash back to the customers for returned goods.

Again, Amazon is a great example of an online marketplace where return is as easy as purchase. A self-service portal can help cancel the order, print the return label, and authorize shipping the order back free of charge. Although it may appear to be expensive on the part of marketplace owners to enable free nonbinding returns, the secret is that a major percentage of items are retained by the customers even if they plan to return the item. Moreover, the customer satisfaction earned by allowing hassle-free returns is valuable for goodwill, which compensates for lost delivery and restocking expenses.

Having described the dynamics of returning purchased items, it's important to note that this process may be less applicable to KIA products because they're nonphysical items. Most of the time, the privileges of delivery and use of streaming assets get terminated as part of canceling an order. Shipping back the item is almost inapplicable for KIA products. In some cases, simple proof of asset deletion may be all that's required. If the KIA asset is delivered, dynamic deletion of encryption keys is another way to disable the use of the product subsequent to any cancellation and cash-back steps.

After-Sales Service

After-sales (aka Post-Sales) service is any service provided after a customer has purchased a product. Examples of after-sales service include warranty services, training, repairs, and upgrades. A prompt and courteous after-sales service usually leads to better customer satisfaction, increased returning customers, repeat sales, and brand loyalty. Although it's a cost center, occasionally after-sales services can also turn out to be a revenue generation method via supplemental fees for training, installation, and repair services.

User Experience

User experience includes the overall shopping experience all the way from identifying the right products through checkout, purchase, payment, and delivery. The single factor of the success of the Amazon marketplace is the quality of its user experience. The one-click purchase method Amazon uses not only simplifies the purchase process, but also makes it easy and quick.

Financing

Financing purchases is common in large-value transactions, such as real estate, automobiles, and expensive equipment and appliances. In the same way as purveyors of such upscale items, many e-commerce marketplaces have started offering similar arrangements to extend temporary credit to prospective buyers. There's no doubt this is an excellent way to attract (and more importantly, retain) customers on the same platform. Many stores offer one-time as well as purchase-based cash-back incentives. The credit offers include store credit cards, installment schemes, and discount coupons for future purchases.

Credit Cards

E-commerce companies usually cooperate with banks and other credit agencies to offer store credit cards to their captive customers. Most departmental shops have their own credit cards, and a similar practice is followed by many online commerce companies. Some years ago, some airline companies like United, Delta, and Southwest started issuing their own credit cards (joining with Visa, Mastercard, or Amex), a practice that was later adopted by Amazon, Walmart, Target, and specialty brands like Home Depot, Best Buy, and Lowe's. These commercial firms also offered additional incentives like money-back guarantees and rebates to incentivize the use of their branded credit cards.

Installment Payments

Installment payment plans are another method of motivating buyers. These plans are also prevalent among traditional shops and marketplaces, and they're often attractive for big-ticket items like furniture, appliances, or expensive electronics. The traders may either charge a finance fee, bill it against the credit cards, or offer them interest-free. Whether it's interest-free or not, an installment scheme based on credit checking is an attractive way to motivate buyers to commit to investing in the goods.

Customizations and Personalization

Personalization of marketplaces can occur at different levels, such as personalized catalogs, personalized shopping experiences (e.g., pre-stored credit card and delivery address), personalized marketing campaigns, personalized recommendations, and personalized communications. There are multiple objectives: improve the customer experience, increase sales via targeted campaigns, and educate consumers and enhance their awareness of specific products and services. Engaging customers with personalization[165] can be crucial to delighting them and inspiring them to return, increasing traffic and boosting future sales. Personalization can significantly improve the sales conversion rate. Some common techniques of personalization are outlined below.

Personalized Catalogs

A personalized catalog is one of the most common first steps. This entails showing the products that potentially are of most interest or relevance to a specific customer. As the customer logs in, data on past searches, purchases, gender, age, profession, and financial status can be employed to come up with a set of products in which that customer may be interested. The catalog can then show the customer these products up front or include the products in a sorted display, which can significantly increase the chance for a sale.

Personalized Ads

Personalized ads include ads shown via related communication, social, and commerce channels that deal with products of interest to a customer. These ads may take the form of emails, messages, or sideline ads on internet sites. This is accomplished by identifying the customer and promoting products to entice them to come to the

---

165 https://www.mckinsey.com/capabilities/growth-marketing-and-sales/our-insights/the-value-of-getting-personalization-right-or-wrong-is-multiplying

e-commerce platform. The difference between a personalized catalog and personalized ads is that ads are displayed or communicated outside the marketplace platform with the intention of bringing customers to the platform, as opposed to showing interesting products to customers who are already signed on to the platform.

Personalized Services

Personalized services include increasing ease of shopping by knowing the customer preferences for shipping address, modes of payment, quantities of products, and qualities of competitive products. This involves storing customer-supplied information for future use. Some other services that can be personalized include searching with intent, prioritization of search results, and offering additional services like warranty and installation, which can be optionally facilitated based on the type of customers and their buying patterns.

As Forrester points out, "organizations that fail to meet buyers' expectations for personalized omnichannel communications risk losing market share to competitors that do[166]."

Personalization Versus Privacy

The more data about a customer that's available, the better the driving-engagement processes can be. Personalization may need detailed, sometimes even intimate, information about the customer. However, collecting data (even if it's available publicly or by other means) on personal tastes and attributes like age, marital status, race, or similar information spotlights the thin boundary between personalization and incursion into privacy. An infamous example[167] is of a woman looking for diapers and baby food who found herself being categorized as pregnant. Consequently, targeted ads or promotional communications related to pregnancy aimed at her could be seen as a violation of her personal privacy.

Marketplace platforms must design and publish clear policies on what data will be gathered by the marketplace platform and how it will be used internally or shared externally. Many social websites and mobile apps have crossed the boundaries of privacy infringement and become subject to litigation and damage compensation. Merely obtaining consent of the customer to collect and use their personal information

---

166 https://www.forrester.com/blogs/conversational-interactions-and-ai-enhancing-the-digital-buying-experience-and-closing-gaps-in-your-sales-process/

167 https://www.forbes.com/sites/kashmirhill/2012/02/16/how-target-figured-out-a-teen-girl-was-pregnant-before-her-father-did/?sh=5647ceed6668

is often not good enough. Responsible platforms should demonstrate a sense of clear moral responsibility by respecting confidentiality of individual privacy and sentiments.

It's heartening to note that major IT and tech companies have started publishing their data policies. For example, Google has outlined how it will be handling personal data by publicly publishing its policies[168]. IBM is in the forefront of devising ethically and legally compliant policies[169] on privacy protection. Microsoft also has committed itself to empower and defend the privacy choices[170] of every person who uses its products and services. Many social platforms like Twitter and Facebook (Meta), and many HR, health care, and retail organizations are now careful to state their policies regarding respect for the privacy and trust of their customers.

Ratings, Reviews, and Recommendations

Collecting, compiling, and publishing product ratings and reviews by end users is an important factor in boosting sales. These reviews can be a simple numerical rating system (1 to 5) or descriptive comments expressing the evaluation or user experience. Reviews can be by paid subject-matter experts, actual end users, or both. Amazon's well-curated five-star rating system has become an industry standard for crowd-sourced product reviews.

Product reviews play a crucial role in increasing sales. A recent survey[171] shows that most consumers globally check reviews online before making purchases, ample proof that facilitating an in-house product review function as part of the marketplace itself can be crucial. A study by Northwestern University[172] says that the conversion rate of a product can increase by 270 percent as it gradually gathers favorable reviews. Product reviews can also be a source of important information for companies to use upstream in the process of defining their marketing and communications strategies and adding value to their unique selling proposition. Most descriptive feedback can provide valuable information about customer expectations, preferences, purchase motivation, product quality, strengths and weaknesses of the services related to a sale and purchase process, ways in which the product is used, feelings related to consumers' experiences, and

168 https://policies.google.com/privacy?hl=en-US

169 https://www.ibm.com/us-en/privacy

170 https://privacy.microsoft.com/en-US/

171 https://cdn2.hubspot.net/hubfs/2749863/2019-trustpilot/The%20Critical%20Role%20of%20Reviews%20in%20Internet%20Trust%20(UK)%20-%20final.pdf

172 https://www.scholars.northwestern.edu/en/publications/the-value-of-online-customer-reviews

comparisons with competitive products. Product reviews can also be used to improve the performance of advertising campaigns.

While reviews are often sourced from the customers, recommendations are a push to promote the products on the platform. Products that are on sale, products newly introduced, or products that may be of interest to the customers can be recommended through emails, pop-ups, and messaging apps. Customer profiling is a key input for such targeted marketing. There are several apps now available to support these functions. Shopify[173], BigCommerce[174], Blueshift[175], and a host of other vendors provide intelligent apps that facilitate product recommendations and reviews. Some of these onsite and in-app recommendations, which display as users browse through products, can significantly increase sales rates.

Advertising

All third-party marketplaces have an opportunity to generate additional revenue via vendor-sponsored ads. This not only increases sales via the platform, but also adds another revenue stream. Amazon makes about $10 billion[176] via ads on its platform. At least one blog reports that more than 60 percent of Alibaba's revenue comes from advertisers[177]. Disney[178] collects nearly $4 billion annually via third-party advertisers. It's common these days to have dominating "sponsored ads" that are highly paid ad spaces monetized by marketplace platforms. Over and above the basic trading functions, an ad engine with multimedia capabilities is an essential component of any successful marketplace.

Marketplace Data Analytics

The need to measure the vitality and growth of marketplace platforms in a continual manner is critical to the success and sustenance of those businesses. Fortunately, plenty of data is generated within platforms themselves, which owners can collect and analyze to sense the pulse of operations and marketplace growth prospects. The most important

---

173 https://apps.shopify.com/

174 https://www.bigcommerce.com/

175 https://blueshift.com/

176 https://www.marketingdive.com/news/amazon-Q3-earnings-holiday-forecast-advertising/635227/

177 https://www.cs-cart.com/blog/how-to-advertise-in-the-online-multi-vendor-marketplace/

178 https://finance.yahoo.com/news/disney-launches-new-ad-tier-why-it-could-be-a-3-billion-opportunity-analyst-202501704.html

performance dimensions of a marketplace platform that need to be measured include financials, market share, customer base and segments, customer behavior, customer sentiments, customer retention, product sales rates, and conversion rate. A number of granular-level metrics prevalent in marketplace analytics can be seen in the guide[179] published by The Signal.

Financials

At a high level, the financials are common across most businesses: the total revenue, the total expenses, and the profit. Although these represent the bottom-line figures that reflect the financial health of the platform as a business, detailed analysis is needed to understand the areas that are shining and lagging. For example, there may be multiple revenue streams, such as sales, ad, and services revenues, as well as membership and listing fees. It's vital to know not only the split of the flow of money from each, but also the trends—growth or decline— of each revenue source. Similarly, expenses need to be measured and analyzed in different buckets and from different angles. Comparing spending against the earnings helps optimize budgets for various types of expenses.

For example, return on ad spend (ROAS) is an important metric for analyzing the results generated from specific types of ads. ROAS being a useful measure usually depends on the brand's target market, ad type, and products[180]. Computing the sourcing expenses of specific products and product segments can provide insights on which ones are more profitable (although profitability is not the only factor in making decisions to source and sell certain products). Other expense categories can include shipping expenses, handling charges, financial charges, and platform operation expenses.

Product and Sales Analysis

While financial numbers reflect the results, the two factors that contribute to results most are products and customers.

Product analytics starts from the simple computation of revenue generated by different types of products and product categories. The analytics should further deepen into specifics like product shelf time, product returns rates, profit margin, cost of acquisition, diversity of sources, diversity of product brands, and product sales volumes.

179 https://mixpanel.com/blog/ultimate-guide-marketplace-analytics/
180 https://e-tailize.com/blog/the-ultimate-marketplace-analytics-guide/

Sales (customer) analytics should measure the processes and functions that enable friction-free sales transactions via the platform. They're influenced somewhat by the price and quality of products; however, they're mainly influenced by the ease and convenience with which the products are bought and sold. The most commonly measured metrics are click-through rate, (the number of clicks necessary before finalizing a sale) and conversion rate (how valuable people find a product or ad). A high conversion rate means the product is appealing and attractive; it serves the right people at the right time and place. It also indicates how effective the process is that motivates the customers to confirm the purchase. A quick delivery, a discount coupon, extra reward points, or even a caution of low stock may encourage prospective customers to buy quickly. These are ways to improve the conversion rate (besides other basic factors of price, product quality, and product reviews).

Customer Data

Knowing your customer is fundamental to any trade. Understanding what they want, their preferences, and their budgets is key to positioning relevant products. For each type of product, from "less-than-a-dollar pens and pencils" to "luxury cars or yachts," there is an audience that is interested in spending money on them. Matching the right products to the right customers depends on analyzing customers and segmenting and targeting them in a focused manner. This requires collecting data about customers. Profiling each customer based on buying patterns, spending patterns, special interests, and seasonal changes is useful to dynamically position sales opportunities. This is the same for both brick-and-mortar businesses and online marketplaces. However, the online marketplaces do have an affinity for capturing the relevant data more intrinsically and automatically. The rest of the job relies on compiling and analyzing the same.

Recap

Digital marketplaces integrate a variety of technical and business functions, from traditional vendor development to technology-driven, touchless digital payments and instant deliveries. A consolidated functional architecture of a typical marketplace is depicted below.

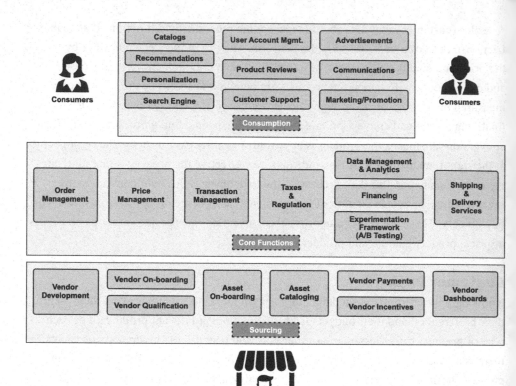

Figure 5.3: Digital Marketplace: Functional Architecture

This functional map of a typical marketplace platform includes three layers. The bottom layer represents the back-end functions, such as vendor development, asset sourcing, cataloging, and vendor payments (billing and invoicing in relation to suppliers). The middle layer is a collection of core functions to support "operations." These cover order management, pricing and price management, shipping and delivery, data logging, collection, analysis, taxes, and finances. The top layer, or front end, represents consumer-facing functions, such as user account management, personalization, user feedback collection, promotions and marketing, third-party ad management, and customer communications. Details of each of these functions are described in the previous sections of this chapter. All three layers need to work together for a healthy growing marketplace, irrespective of the type of assets the marketplace handles.

Many advanced technology components come into play—such as immersive user experience for product cataloging, AI model–centric personalization, search engines, targeted marketing, secured payment services, and massive infrastructure based on advanced cloud technology—to support transactions, users, product contents, and associated ecosystems. Besides the communication and transportation sectors, the online trade has spun off many enabling technologies that are reused elsewhere. The impact of online trading and technology spin-offs are mutually supportive. The need for scaled online transactions is driving new innovations while the digital transformation creates new market economies as well as triggers new ways of buying and selling.

CHAPTER 6

REVENUE MODELS FOR KIA MARKETPLACES

"To know values is to know the meaning of the market."
—Charles Dow

Introduction

Generating value or revenue while simultaneously creating an influential social and cultural fabric is the key objective of a marketplace. There can be many different—and often concurrent—revenue generation models, based on the nature of commodities of the marketplace, the type of transactions allowed, and the types of stakeholders. These include traditional direct sales, sales-related services, listing fees, onboarding fees, transaction-dependent revenue, revenue from associated services, membership fees, advertisement revenue, and even open business models where the assets are exchanged free of cost.

In this chapter, some of the popular schemes of revenue generation are described with examples of models appropriate in different scenarios.

Outright Sales

This is the most common and well-understood pricing model, where product ownership is transferred for a fixed or negotiable one-time payment. Sometimes these prices are negotiable, as it can be for big-ticket items—homes, automobiles, artworks, and big equipment. Variations of this pricing model include a fixed price with a one-time payment, a fixed price paid in installments, a negotiated price, a bid price (i.e., an auction in which the highest bidder gets the item), and an entitled price (e.g., blanket negotiations for B2B or B2C). Rebates and sale prices are additional considerations of the outright sale pricing model. The main characteristics of this pricing model are that the transaction is closed as the payment is done and the item is delivered (other than handling potential cancellation of the purchase order before the item is delivered or return of the item after delivery). Other touch points are any installation, training, or warranty services that are part of the sales contract or included in the price paid.

There are some variations of the outright sales pattern. Tiered pricing, volume-based pricing, graduated pricing, and flat-rate-per-seat are some examples. In tiered pricing, prices can represent levels that enable the unit cost to change with quantity or usage. This lets sellers offer lower rates for customers who use more quantities within a prescribed period. With volume-based pricing, the subscription item is billed at the tier corresponding to the amount of usage at the end of the period. Like volume pricing, graduated pricing charges are based on usage in each tier instead of applying a single price to all usage.

Some companies name products differently, based on the pricing scheme prescribed. The product description is common; however, the model may differ based on the pricing model chosen. "Flat plus per-seat" is another model of pricing structure that includes both a base fee and additional per-seat pricing. One product may serve as the flat base price and the other product represents the variable per-seat pricing.

Subscription Fee

The intrinsic nature of KIAs makes them suitable to be offered as a service. The subscription model may resemble the pay-as-you-use model below; however, the main difference is that subscription can be a fixed, regularly paid fee for a specific duration while pay-as-you-use in its purest form charges only for the quantity of consumption during the billing period. Monthly or yearly subscription is common for music and movie marketplaces and education or training services. The subscription service can be for unlimited use or different levels of service based on the subscription fee.

Pay-as-You-Use

The pay-as-you-use model is prevalent in the utility industry. Use of a product or service is metered, and customers are charged each time they use the service. The pay-as-you-use model doesn't assume a fixed monthly or annual fee; users pay for what they use, whereas subscription typically has set pricing tiers.

A variation of the pay-as-you-use model is the pay-as-you-go model, in which a customer with limited funds can pay for equipment like solar panels or mobile phones over time. Leasing high-value equipment that can potentially be shared with multiple users is also a variation of the same revenue model. In another scenario, the company provider finances the purchase of the equipment, but ownership is transferred to the customer at the end of the repayment contract, which is different from pay-as-you-use, in which ownership is not transferred.

From one side, the main advantage of the pay-as-you-use model is that the consumers need to pay only for what they use, which helps when demand fluctuates. On the other hand, consumers may have to pay high costs during frequent-use periods because fixed pricing is often not guaranteed. For providers, this model makes it easier to market the value they provide, and they are able to control a more flexible price. However, as happens in utility services, the providers need to take risks during unpredictable revenue fluctuations, especially when consumption levels are lower, so a way to accurately meter the consumption and support a relatively complicated billing process is needed. To offset the risk, sometimes these models will include a fixed fee or minimum charge and a metering equipment rental fee, along with a variable charge based on consumption levels.

Membership Fees

A membership model is a type of business plan in which individuals pay a recurring fee to access the value an organization creates. This model may also involve different membership levels (e.g., gold, silver, or platinum), which have specific levels of service or privileges. The membership model can also be combined with other models, an example being the Amazon Prime membership, in which the membership doesn't provide free services but offers privileges like special prices and free and expedited delivery. The membership model is more applicable in scenarios[181] like these:

---

181 https://www.wildapricot.com/blog/membership-model#7-benefits-of-using-a-membership-model

- Clubs (music or movie club, tennis club, gym club)
- Professional associations (writing association, engineering association, nursing association)
- Nonprofits (foundations, churches, charities)
- Businesses (online courses, Costco, Amazon Prime)

The advantages of the membership model are many. It is simple and easy to manage, the platform owners get a set of committed stakeholders that makes it easier to market goods and services, it is easier to understand the user dynamics, it lowers business operating and marketing costs, it gives members access to exclusive data, and it simplifies the process of diversifying the product suite. Although it ensures a stable revenue stream, itis difficult for this model to scale up and increase the membership span. For the consumers, the fee is predictable; however, there is less control over the quality of products and services available.

Barter System

The barter system, although old, remains prevalent in different forms and is still a good system of give and take for sharing resources, making it suitable and sustainable in many situations. In the KIA online marketplace, barter may appear in some scenarios— for example, one gets free services or points for doing a review of products or watching an ad. The main issue with a barter system is that the valuation of different types of goods and services (their fair market value) may be difficult to determine without a common basis of understanding and acceptance. Before the existence of the concepts of stores and currencies (all the way back in 9000 BC), the purchase of goods was completed by trading one product or service for another[182]. In many cases, this meant using animals as a form of payment. Of course, defining the price of an item as a certain number of cows and sheep reflects a similarity with modern currencies in the sense that they are countable and can be transported and transferred. One difference, though, is that these bartered items were of some intrinsic use, as opposed to currency which, once exchanged, still needs to be exchanged for some other goods of utility.

The Internal Revenue Service (IRS)[183] (the U.S. federal government tax agency) recognizes barter transactions but then needs to compute the dollar value of those

---

182 https://aifora.com/en/blog-en/the-history-of-pricing-from-the-barter-system-to-dynamic-pricing/

183 https://www.irs.gov/

transactions. When it isn't possible to accurately calculate the value, in some situations the bartered goods are reported based on their carrying value[184].

The barter system is still prevalent in a C2C (customer-to-customer) scenario, especially for services like babysitting, lawn mowing, tutoring, ridesharing, home stays, and moving assistance. In some companies, some of the perks offered can also be considered as compensation, such as security services, chauffeur services, or tax-preparation services offered to the employees that are, in fact, in return for their work or other services rendered to the company.

Trading advertisement rights[185] is another example. Here, one company sells its available ad space to another company in exchange for the right to advertise on the second company's space. These can be for television airtime rights, internet advertisements, radio rights, billboards, or various other types of media.

Donations for Public or Free Offerings

Many public (free) marketplaces survive by using voluntary payments or donations. Examples are Khan Academy, Wikipedia, and National Public Radio (NPR). Users who are broadminded and generous voluntarily donate money in exchange for the quality services they get from these not-for-profit marketplace owners. These marketplaces also obtain grants from charitable trusts or government. While this isn't a dependable monetization model, many socially conscious platforms adopt it because their objective is to provide free services to the public.

While the donation model of raising income or generating revenue stream is unpredictable and not scalable inorganically, it's still a viable model, depending on the content and services the platforms provide and the audience to which they are addressed. For example, Wikipedia, a trusted source of information on various topics, people, places, and events, raises about $160 million through donations. Theirs is a soft and gentle marketing campaign for money, as opposed to those of many other charitable organizations. The secret of survival of such platforms is keeping the costs minimal through volunteer work and accepting only limited sponsored ads from typically noncontroversial sponsors.

Individual contributions are the largest source of revenue for public media entities, which primarily come through membership donations to local stations[186]. NPR in the

184 https://www.investopedia.com/terms/c/carryingvalue.asp
185 https://www.investopedia.com/ask/answers/101314/what-are-some-examples-barter-transactions.asp
186 https://cpb.org/aboutcpb

U.S. is an example of a news service that uses both traditional and online streaming platforms. NPR gets a significant chunk of its operational money from public and charitable-foundation donations and corporate sponsorships. It also receives a small percentage of its budget from federal and state agencies. NPR supports "soft ads" in return for monetary contributions from "responsible and socially conscious" businesses and professionals.

Donation models always come with restrictions on the way the business is operated, such as making its policies clear and known up front and not becoming involved in any types of profit-making or other controversial connections and activities.

Associated Services: Tools, Consulting, Training

For any marketplace, depending on the type of products or commodities being transacted, there are several related or associated services. Examples are banks offering credit cards and insurance, auto dealers offering financing, Home Depot offering installation and training, real-estate agencies offering mortgage products, and restaurants offering catering and cooking classes. This model of revenue generation is prevalent even in traditional commercial establishments.

In general, most manufacturers, suppliers, and marketplaces offer different types of services. Service revenues often accompany product sales or other types of revenue streams, such as:

- Implementation fees that include software and hardware configuration, installation, parameters setting, operating trial runs and demos for customers, training of customer personnel, maintenance services, or similar functions
- Consulting fees for any technical help, advice, training, custom development, and system integrations
- Customer support fees for answering questions, bug fixes, repairs, upgrades, and preventive maintenance
- Customization fees for services such as extending software, additional development work with other KIA assets, developing special interfaces, and any type of specific work unique to a particular customer

It is evident that services revenue could be a significant part of revenue in many sectors, such as automobiles, computer hardware and software, and those involving large equipment like aircraft or chemical plants.

Associated services serve three main purposes:

1. Increase traffic to a portal because the content and single-stop shopping experience will attract more traffic

2. The sale of tools and contracts involved with the services will be another opportunity for the vendors to make additional money and in turn enable transactional fees by the marketplace host

3. Because many vendors may have other tools and services as offerings, this becomes an additional channel for revenue generation

To improve the monetization of the marketplace and increase its stickiness (a tendency for prices in product markets to adjust slowly in response to changes in supply and demand), the marketplace should provide associated services that:

- Enable marketplace customers to use these assets directly within their analytic applications

- Give asset providers the capability to safely store and enrich their assets

- Enable a community of "intermediaries" that provide consulting and implementation services on top of data assets and bridge the "implementation gap" between providers and consumers

The KIA upselling and cross-selling opportunities are even more diverse and rich. For example, in an AI marketplace, besides trading AI models and offering Model as a Service (MaaS), a marketplace can offer several related engineering services. These may include model validation, model deployment, model version management, model comparison, and application development using AI models. These services may be offered as part of the platform by third-party vendors or by the platform's hosting organization.

A data marketplace can support such additional services as data cleansing and curation, data analysis, data rendering, data protection and privacy, data storage, and data archival. In an advertising marketplace, ad analytics, ad placement, and ad customization services are typical. In an app marketplace, relevant additional services include providing development and test platforms, application deployment, and application testing.

Advertisements

Advertisements make good sense wherever people gather and wherever people pay attention. E-commerce platforms are no exception. In fact, in addition to the online catalog, advertisements of competitive products and paid advertisements by vendors are essential for any online marketplace. Digital ads are a world of their own. The placement of an ad and the sharing of the ad-space real estate are important design criteria. Ad promotion algorithms are prevalent and are used by many vendors to make their products surface at the top of a list when potential customers browse through catalogs.

Many online platforms survive only on ad revenue. Many platforms that offer free services for product reviews, price comparisons, education and training, and news services rely heavily on sponsored advertisements. The well-known model is that of Google. This behemoth company generates more than $200 billion through digital ads[187], which is the bulk of the company's overall revenue. Meta (formerly Facebook) ad earnings reached $100 billion[188] in 2021. Digital ads have already generated more than 65 percent of all ad revenues and continue to grow.

Although collecting money for ads is an age-old business practice, it remains a complex combination of art and science when it comes to online platforms. Google has perfected that art. It incentivizes not only the content providers but also the content consumers. Data regarding the types of ads, the placement of ads, and the consumption of ads are all important factors. These key metrics are dynamically collected and analyzed to optimize ad effectiveness as well as to maximize revenue. Of course, customization and personalization of ads and determining the mode of delivery are also critical factors.

Financing: Credit Cards, Gift Cards, Long-Term Credits

Financing and credit offerings either through custom credit cards or company-sponsored installment payments are common to all marketplace vendors. Amazon and Target credit cards are good examples of card use in the consumer marketplace, although large enterprises often extend financing to enable million-dollar purchases. Such supplier-provider financing helps in two major ways. It's an incentive to buyers who may not have enough resources to make full payment immediately. For sellers, it can lead to more sales as well as additional income from finance charges. Many marketplaces offer a nominal rebate or "small percentage of payback" to encourage buyers to use their financing or credit cards because of this dual benefit of increased sales and potential additional revenue through interest payments.

Even corporate B2B purchases may also include optional financing schemes. Many enterprises like Boeing, IBM, Microsoft, and many auto manufacturers offer long-

187 https://www.statista.com/statistics/266249/advertising-revenue-of-google/

188 https://www.oberlo.com/statistics/facebook-ad-revenue

term financing to their customers as an incentive to buy their products and services. This Original Equipment Manufacturer (OEM) financing is again a win-win scenario in which the suppliers can encourage customers to buy their products with nominal or no-interest finance charges. For example, Microsoft states[189] that its financing "helps facilitate adoption of Microsoft's intelligent cloud, intelligent edge solutions with flexible payment options designed to address customer's business and financial requirements. With payment solutions, customers can simplify cloud adoption by accepting funding for software and services, structure payments to meet customers' business requirements, and minimize up-front payments and pay as you deploy your IT solution and realize benefits."

IBM[190] supports innovative payment models—such as payment plans, leasing, and flexible payment options—as an important way to support their organization's digital transformation.

Leasing

Leasing is another financial model that may be considered as a variation of financing, except that the ownership is not fully transferred at any time. Leasing is a common revenue model in trading of high-value appliances, equipment, automobiles, and real estate, in which the assets are temporarily given to customers for their possession and use.

The leasing model[191] enables customers to pay the suppliers periodically for the time-limited use of a product without having to own the product. The company takes care of the maintenance of its physical assets, insurance costs, and other usual expenses.

Under the leasing business model, a company purchases, owns, or manufactures a product and then leases it to a customer for a periodic fee. Leasing transactions normally involve three parties: the seller, the buyer (lessee), and the financier (lessor). The seller may or may not retake ownership of the item once the leasing contract has ended.

This business model makes the leased products more accessible to consumers without requiring a huge down payment or long-term commitment and reaches a larger market when the price of the product is important—mostly costly equipment, luxury

189 https://download.microsoft.com/download/3/9/0/390DF0B3-8B15-4E65-AF5E-71A7280E7682/Microsoft-Financing-Program-FAQ-Customer_en-US.pdf

190 https://www.ibm.com/financing

191 https://learn.marsdd.com/article/the-leasing-revenue-model-and-leasing-arrangements/

cars, or portions of real estate. Leasing also ensures regular income for the lessor, as the lessee is required to pay periodically an amount agreed upon between the two parties. Also, the lessor has the advantage of retaining ownership of the product, which ensures additional income in the event of resale. For lessees, this model is advantageous when what they rent costs more than they use. Instead of having to buy the property, they pay a fixed sum at regular intervals. The disadvantage for lessees is that the money paid results in no claim to ownership. For the lessor, the risk of costs of maintenance of the property, insurance, depreciation, and loss of value due to technological advances are possible disadvantages. Rental businesses account for about $2 trillion in business worldwide[192], especially widespread in sectors where the price of goods is consequential.

Committed Spends

Committed spend[193] refers to the annual spending to which a business commits, as laid out in a broader agreement or contract valid for a specific time called the "commitment period." There can be many committed-spend scenarios. For the purchaser, these include those that can be associated with one main order that has already been executed, a general agreement with a total budget designated to buy a category of products and services, or a high-level agreement to a pay-as-you-use arrangement with special price agreements for a fixed future time period. For the supplier, it amounts to a more or less guaranteed revenue from that customer. For the customer, this means a preferred supplier with a negotiated price advantage. Actual purchase orders cannot be issued up front as the size and time of demand may not be known in advance.

Military and government procurements often fall into this type of committed-purchase contract. Another example is when a company buys a machine for $40,000 and issues a purchase order to pay for a maintenance contract for $2,000 in each of the next three years, the entire $46,000 is a committed cost because the company has already bought the machine and has a legal obligation to pay for the maintenance. Another example can be a large enterprise that makes a software purchase with a minimum and maximum number of licenses. As employees onboard, payments increase to add licenses.

192 https://www.thebusinessresearchcompany.com/report/real-estate-rental-global-market-report
193 https://cloud.google.com/billing/docs/how-to/cud-analysis-spend-based

Marketplace KPIs

There can be different dimensions[194] by which the success of a marketplace can be measured:

- Usage metrics track customer visits to the platform (such as monthly visitors, bounce rate, and time spent).

- Transaction metrics help purveyors understand the health of their marketplace mechanics. Examples are liquidity, provider-to-customer ratio, and repeat purchase ratio.

- Financial health is indicated by the business metrics, such as gross merchandise value, customer acquisition cost, and customer lifetime value.

A common way to track user activity is to measure monthly active users. Typically, this is done by counting the number of unique users who have visited the site at least once during a certain period.

Bounce rate measures the percentage of visitors who enter a site and leave right away rather than staying to engage with the site in some way. Time spent on the site shows user interest in the platform, which may lead to transactions.

Liquidity is defined as "the percentage of listings that lead to transactions within a certain time period." Examples of provider liquidity are the proportion of total stock sold in each period, or for a hotelier, the proportion of rooms booked each night. Customer liquidity means the probability of a visit leading to a transaction. A simple but approximate way to measure this is to calculate how many customer visits happen in each month and how many transactions happen in the same period. In many cases, customer liquidity is more than provider liquidity.

A marketplace's inner dynamics are indicated by another metric called provider-to-customer ratio or the buyer-to-seller ratio. It is the number of customers that one provider can serve.

Another interesting metric is how big a percentage of a site's transactions are repeat purchases (i.e., from people who have already made purchases on the site). In a way, this is a customer-retention indicator. A high retention assures protection of existing revenue and indicates additional effort can result in growth with new users. It is also an indicator of the customer Net Promoter Score (NPS), a customer loyalty and satisfaction measurement.

Business metrics aim to answer questions related to a business's revenue, profitability, and customer acquisition success.

194 https://www.sharetribe.com/academy/measure-your-success-key-marketplace-metrics/

Gross Merchandise Volume (GMV) means the total sales value of the products or services sold via a marketplace during a specific period. This is an important metric of marketplace growth.

Customer acquisition cost (CAC) means the price paid to acquire a new customer. In an ideal situation, this number is close to zero. Each customer refers a site to at least one new potential customer, and the audience grows organically without the marketplace owner having to do anything.

Customer lifetime value (CLV) is a metric calculating a customer's total value over the customer's lifetime. An exact valuation for this metric may require a long period of time and can be tricky to estimate because it depends on how long a marketplace is able to retain a customer, how many repeat purchases the customer is expected to make, and the size of the customer's average transaction. Customer lifetime value is also a critical KPI that demonstrates the total amount of revenue expected from each customer. As a rule of thumb, customer lifetime value should be higher than customer acquisition cost.

Recap

Revenue models are varied in size and shape, and each comes with its own pros and cons. One important aspect is that a marketplace doesn't necessarily stick to one type of revenue model. Many platforms adopt a combination of multiple business models that ensure stability, growth, and sustenance. Moreover, newer revenue streams are always invented by ingenious business teams, based on market demand, consumer sentiments, and technology evolution. Long-term financial health is the foundation of the success of marketplaces, just like any other business.

CHAPTER 7

AUTOMATION AND SCALING OF KIA MARKETPLACES

"Automation applied to an inefficient operation will magnify the inefficiency."
—Bill Gates

Introduction

Marketplaces become viable business entities with incoming profits only when they reach a critical size in sales volume and numbers of vendors and consumers. A plan and roadmap for scaling up the platform to reach critical thresholds and sustain growth are necessary, particularly in the early stages. The best way, as in all cases, is to automate the operations so that scaling is sustainable and sufficient to ensure revenue growth and profitability. This chapter discusses areas where automation is necessary and shows how to measure success in terms of a set of industry-defined KPIs. The chapter also describes tools and techniques needed to automate the different steps.

Automation Is the Key to Scaling

Success in marketplace operations is dependent on being able to manage scale with both products and customers. Although customers bring in the revenue, their engagement and resulting transactions happen only when a rich set of products is available in the marketplace and the platform supports a delightful user experience. This is a double-sided coin.

The initial focus in most current marketplaces is on enabling a large set of vendors and products to be made available to consumers. Enabling products or services on a platform and updating marketplace information are of paramount importance, and automation plays a key role in this. Examples are platforms like Amazon, eBay, Craigslist, TaskRabbit, and YouTube, where the richness and diversity of products and services on offer are the main attraction for consumers. This means the products need to be categorized and displayed appropriately based on many contextual factors, including personal preferences. Availability of products and service providers needs to be kept up to date. In many matching platforms like Airbnb, Uber, TaskRabbit, the availability of services and providers may change by the minute. Leah Busque, founder of TaskRabbit, says, "In any marketplace, it's critical that the supply side have the tools they need to scale and be successful. Otherwise, the marketplace will be tenuous and may not support an influx of supply and demand."[195]

To provide a positive experience to consumers, the supply side needs to be dynamic, agile, and diverse.

The supply side tasks benefitting from automation include vetting the vendors, collecting and cataloging the products or services, categorizing offerings, personalizing displays, providing an easy way to find and access the products, dynamic pricing,

195 https://medium.com/@labunleashed/the-anatomy-of-a-marketplace-16b9d4ee8174

uality checking and crowd-rating of products, delivery of products and services on ime, royalty payments to vendors, and billing and related taxation management.

Quality and Privacy of KIAs in Marketplaces

Privacy considerations appear in many ways in KIA marketplaces. Sensitivity of data— whether it's personal, transactional, or device-generated—is extensively debated and is an active topic of research[196]. Privacy preservation is equally critical in other types of KIA transactions, such as AI models, ads, photos, videos, and courseware. Privacy-related considerations—such as factual correctness, ownership, lineage, bias, and moral and legal implications—become complex because KIA assets are so new, diverse, and non-standardized, as well as being sourced from a larger set of producers in comparison with traditional physical goods like electronics, books, vegetables, stationery, or groceries. Each of these KIA products appears in different formats, supplied by a multitude of real and fake creators and producers, and is subject to manipulation more easily with numerous readily available tools. The governance of the KIA products warrants automated tools that can manage large-scale assets.

The following sections cover some of these issues that affect the different components of privacy and accuracy concepts.

Ownership and Lineage

For all marketplace assets, information such as who produced it, who owns it, and what has happened in its life so far are important data that every customer wants to know before deciding to buy. For most traditional products, the product includes labels that indicate by whom and when it was created, how it was packaged, the ingredients of the product, and any checks or certifications (FDA/FCC) that attest to product quality. KIA products are relatively new to the industry, and the practices, regulations, and expectations of such metadata are still emerging. In fact, given the cognitive nature of KIA products, the importance of ownership, descriptions of how it was created and handled, as well as who owns it are particularly important in establishing asset credibility. It is the responsibility of the marketplace platform owners to make sure they have verified, collected, and recorded this information on the data, models, and videos that they are cataloging and selling via their platform. Automation and quality management go hand in hand with an increase in the volume and dynamic nature of these assets.

---

196 https://www.gartner.com/en/legal-compliance/insights/data-privacy-compliance

Trust and Bias

The very nature of KIA products makes them extremely sensitive to trust and bias considerations. This is because of the difficulty of determining the authenticity and integrity of these assets, as opposed to traditionally traded commodities. For traditional products, the functions and features are far more well defined and familiar to the consumers, whereas KIAs are newer, voluminous, dynamic, and more influential. Practices and processes for testing their correctness and completeness are still evolving and have not matured. This is a major impediment to scaling the inventory on these marketplace platforms. For example, bias in data resulting from improper collection or careless handling during any subsequent transformation stages can cause serious issues when an asset is intended for building models or being employed in critical decision-making. Verification of the authenticity of an image, video, or audio asset requires complex tools and a framework, especially when such assets are being sourced by varied vendors in a marketplace. Present lack of standards, the still-evolving nature of best practices and certification procedures, and the ease with which adulteration or corruption of KIA products is possible all present immense challenges to the adoption and scaling of KIA marketplaces.

The key aspects of provenance, security, trust, fairness, ethics, explainability, auditability, and regulation (e.g., export restrictions) related to models are key issues for AI marketplaces. Skepticism related to gender discrimination and racial bias also stands in the way of trusting the decisions and recommendations made by AI models, which in turn inhibits their widespread use. These challenges point to how important it is for an AI marketplace to embrace trust, fairness, ethics, and interpretability as its core tenets.

Below is a list of tools offered by IBM for determining AI fairness, explainability, transparency, robustness, and uncertainty quantifications.

- AI Fairness 360[197]—Identifies protected attributes, offers bias mitigation
- AI Explainability 360 [198]—Comprehends how machine-learning models predict labels
- AI FactSheets 360—Assembles documentation about an AI model's features, such as purpose, performance, and data sets

---

197 https://ai-fairness-360.org/
198 https://ai-explainability-360.org/

- Adversarial Robustness 360 Toolbox (ART)[199]—Defends against inference, poisoning, extraction, and evasion and also verifies AI models' resistance to adversarial attacks

- Fairness Monitoring with IBM Watson OpenScale—Fairness-detection techniques in IBM Watson OpenScale determine whether outcomes are fair or not for a monitored group

- Uncertainty Quantification 360 (UQ360)[200]—Quantifies the uncertainty of machine-learning predictions, with the goal of improving transparency and trust in AI

Amazon, Google, and Microsoft offer services for determining model interpretability and fairness. The section below details the offerings from each of these companies with regard to responsibility and explainability.

- Explainable AI from Google provides AI explanations in forms that include AutoML tables, AI platform predictions, and AI platform notebooks.

- Azureml-Interpret[201] from Microsoft provides an Azure Machine Learning wrapper for running InterpretML techniques developed in the Interpret-Community. Fairlearn's open-source package assesses systems' fairness and mitigates unfairness. Differential privacy and confidential AI are also some techniques used by Microsoft to enable trustworthy AI.

- Amazon SageMaker Clarify[202] can detect potential bias and helps explain the predictions that the machine-learning models make. Amazon's joint research center announcement with University of Southern California (USC) in January 2021 to develop novel approaches to privacy-preserving ML solutions clearly indicates the company's commitment to responsible AI.

Legal and Moral Issues

Legal and moral issues are important to trading in all marketplaces. It is well known there are concerns about selling and buying tobacco and liquor products, as well as much-debated proposals for restrictions on transactions related to guns, explosives, or harmful drugs. Even for many common goods, there are restrictions imposed by

199 https://adversarial-robustness-toolbox.org/

200 https://dl.acm.org/doi/fullHtml/10.1145/3493700.3493767

201 https://learn.microsoft.com/en-us/azure/machine-learning/how-to-machine-learning-interpretability?view=azureml-api-2

202 https://docs.aws.amazon.com/sagemaker/latest/dg/clarify-fairness-and-explainability.html

governmental and local entities as well as professional-group prescribed practices that must be taken into account. Sometimes religious considerations (in some countries) and general societal moral guidelines can affect certain types of trading platforms. KIA marketplaces aren't free from such restrictions, monitoring, and regulation. Many social media platforms have started fact-checking, as well as verifying foul language and inappropriate content. Government-imposed restrictions such as those on data transportation (e.g., the E.U.'s General Data Protection Regulation, or GDPR), data privacy, and data usage may be relevant. For example, many financial institutions are not allowed to commercially exploit the data related to their customers. Data-retention policies are also governed by organizational objectives and governmental regulations. Marketplaces have started encountering increasing legal governance rules as they catalog and sell KIA products.

Moral issues in dealing with KIA entities are a newly emerging talking point. The purpose of collecting, storing, transmitting, and using KIAs, images, videos, and personal data as a means of trading potentially dangerous information (anything that may instigate or help criminal activity or present a danger to society or the environment) are considered undesirable trading practices in KIA marketplaces. Checking for proper usage of transacted KIA assets is sensitive and often confusing because what is seemingly proper for one party may be considered unfair or improper by other parties. Many leaders in the industry, society, and political parties have started discussing what should be considered proper and improper, and it will likely take some time before all parties can agree on some common practices and guidelines.

Securing KIA Assets in Marketplaces

Securing products in a marketplace has an additional dimension when it comes to KIAs. Unlike other e-commerce platforms for physical products, KIA products are often not only cataloged on the platform, but also stored there. This makes such assets vulnerable to theft and, more crucially, corruption or damage. Marketplaces must take care to preserve the integrity of KIA products.

Security in Software

The December 2020 SUNBURST cyberattack[203] on SolarWinds' software-building environment illustrates a disturbing new reality for the software industry and illuminates the increasingly sophisticated threats that can be made by outside the

---

203 https://en.wikipedia.org/wiki/2020_United_States_federal_government_data_breach

ɔoundaries of nations to the supply chains and infrastructure that are foundational for ɔnline marketplaces.

Emerging standards, such as the Supply-chain Levels for Software Artifacts ˌSLSA)[204] and the Cloud Native Computing Foundation's (CNCF's) software supply-ɔhain best practices whitepaper, take this state of play into account and recommend that ɨll artifacts with a feasible path to reproducibility use it. Key principles for supply-ɔhain security and steps for each include:

- Trust: Every step in a supply chain should be "trustworthy," assured by a combination of cryptographic attestation and verification.

- Automation: Automation is critical to supply-chain security and can significantly reduce the possibility of human error and configuration drift.

- Clarity: The build environments used in a supply chain should be clearly defined, with limited scope.

- Mutual authentication: All entities operating in the supply-chain environment must be required to mutually authenticate using hardened authentication mechanisms with regular key rotation. The basic idea of a Software Bill of Materials (SBOM) is simple. Every software application should have a bill of materials that lists all application components. This mirrors the bills of material that all electronics products in the physical world have. Two prominent organizations—the Linux Foundation and the Open Web Application Security Project (OWASP)—have SBOM technologies: Software Package Data Exchange (SPDX)[205] and Cyclone.

Data Security

Given the stringent laws concerning data privacy and data movement (GDPR and similar), any data marketplace should make sure all transactions that go through the platform adhere to local, country, and international regulations. Adequate tools for data masking and data depersonalization should also be offered as a value-added service to data providers.

Assuring the provenance of data is a critical issue to ensure the authenticity, ownership chain, and rights associated with transactions in whole or in part against that data. This disclosure must be a requirement for sellers so that buyers understand the data's provenance and the rights that can be conveyed to them. The operator of a data

---

204 https://slsa.dev/
205 https://spdx.dev/

marketplace must also review and attest to the provenance of any data that it allows to be stored within and cataloged on its platform.

Tooling to support prevention of fraudulent usage (volumes of transactions, combinations of data being procured) is also critical to make sure the usage of data purchased through the platform is ethical and legal.

Data Provider Data Provenance Attestation(s)

As part of the account registration to a data marketplace, if clients identify themselves as a data provider (DP), then the terms and conditions (T&C) management component identifies and presents the required T&Cs associated with data provenance attestations(s), including but not limited to:

- Agreement of the DP to document ownership of all data assets referenced by catalog entries in the data marketplace.

- Agreement of the DP to provide data provenance attestation(s) for all data entries published in the catalog of the data marketplace.

- Agreement of the DP to update and recertify data provenance attestation(s) for all data entries that are changed in the data marketplace's catalog.

Clients who identify themselves as DPs need to agree to these terms and conditions as part of the account registration process. The T&C-management component provides a capability for data marketplaces to create and update the specifics of the contracts and track each client's acceptance of such contracts.

Importance and Challenges for Data Distribution and Sharing

There are different risks in data distribution and use because of potential data leaks, unauthorized data usage and management, and intellectual property (IP) and privacy violations. It is essential to evaluate the risks and mitigate them with appropriate contractual and technical measures:

- Concerns over damage by unauthorized use of data
- Government initiatives related to data collection and distribution
- Different worldwide regulations of data usage and data privacy (PCI, GDPR, CCPA, and similar)
- Data ownership

- Data sovereignty, especially important now that data is subject to the laws of the country in which it's located

- Data usage and competition policy

- Data destruction or deletion of data if required by law and regulations (the rules for destruction or deletion of data being stipulated, with evidence of the destruction or deletion available as necessary)

- Methods of categorizing data

- Data curation and active management of data sets

Data distribution models can be accomplished through various technical approaches, as does the authorization and management of access and use. These are a few examples of data distribution models:

- Data provisioning (from one party to another) in which the data provider retains and hosts the data, providing controlled access to other parties

- Multi-stakeholder data generation through the participation of multiple stakeholders to create new data through the participation of multiple parties

- Data sharing generated with participation of multiple stakeholders (many business parties provide data to a platform, which aggregates, stores, processes, and analyzes the data to share such data through the platform)

With the typical issues related to so-called data ownership—how to handle derived data (data that is newly generated through processing, analysis, editing, or integration of any acquired data) or when the contracting party creates (processes or integrates) new data—attention should be given to the handling of personal information and cross-border transactions.

There are also legal aspects regarding AI-based software, including liability that might arise in connection with development and use, as well as rights of ownership. Development of AI-based software depends on the data used for training, and it's difficult to predict the outcome, potentially causing disputes between the parties regarding performance or data model accuracy. Some customers believe that if the models are trained from their data, then they own the models. This is a larger topic for discussion and often involves other controversial issues and questions around AI usage. For example, if an AI-based model developed by Participant A (a vendor) after provision of data from Participant B (a data provider) causes damage to Participant C (a user of a resulting service), the question arises of who is responsible. Is the data at fault? Or is it the service, model, or program that was developed based on that data?

An enterprise data marketplace must carefully identify the rights and liabilities associated with the offering, sale, and subsequent use of all items that are cataloged and offered through the marketplace, including data, models, tools, applications, and services. Consumers of data, derivative insights, or models offered through the marketplace must have access to the provenance of such an item, attested to by the data providers for a given offering.

Security of AI Models

As enterprise-grade AI models are deployed in hybrid multi-cloud environments, zero trust has become a major motivation for building secure and attack-resilient AI models. Business stakeholders need access to data and must perform AI computing in zero-trust environments while retaining complete control over the security of their data and intellectual property (IP) with absolute guarantees against leakage. Using AI models that are resilient to evasion, poisoning, model theft, and data leakage attacks while leveraging data across the enterprise has become a top priority.

Several broad directions in innovations to secure AI models are being pursued by large AI tech companies as well as the larger technical community, and capabilities have started emerging to enable building resilient AI solutions.

One thrust is in building resilience within the AI model or its metadata. For example, research in adversarial robustness is addressing robustness against evasion, poisoning, model theft, and data leakage attacks. A second area of pursuit is the development of metadata tagging (e.g., fact sheets), which captures results of a readiness evaluation exercise that grades the AI model on its robustness against adversarial attacks[206]. A third focus is in building capabilities for AI to work with encrypted or secured data, such as federated learning, privacy-preserving ML using differential privacy techniques, homomorphic encryption, and trusted execution environments[207][208]. This is an extremely active area of research, with leading industrial labs and academia pursuing various threads under the general umbrella of security and AI.

Making the KIA Marketplaces User-Friendly

One of the major factors of success of the Amazon marketplace is the ease and quickness of locating the right product and completing the transaction. Often,

206 https://researcher.watson.ibm.com/researcher/view_group.php?id=9571
207 https://researcher.watson.ibm.com/researcher/view_group.php?id=10276,
208 https://arxiv.org/abs/2108.04417

convenience and the good impression of customers overshadow the price of the commodities, meaning customers are ready to pay a bit more for better service, which is sometimes referred to as "Lexus-level service." This user experience stems from different aspects of the customers who are interacting and transacting with the marketplace, and the following sections briefly cover some of those functional areas. 'Better than the best," and "do it right from start" aren't mere slogans for customer experience but essential ingredients for customer retention, loyalty, and appreciation.

Product Display and Catalog

It is not enough to have good products with the right price. The products need to be known to the customer, and they need to be organized and displayed in a manner that's best suited for different customer segments, geographies, languages, ages, financial statuses, and cultures. A scalable but easily manageable and browsable catalog is the face of the marketplace. As discussed earlier in the marketplace functions chapter, modern catalogs need to be dynamic, personalized, and attractive to users. Creating catalogs is both a science and an art that's fully engulfed with technology and data-driven approaches. Showing the new deals and latest product additions, as well as displaying products of interest to customers are already common in many marketplaces. However, scaling to massive product sets and coping with a large diversity of products are challenges that need to be anticipated and addressed at the design and architecture levels. Translating into local languages, currencies, and units of measurements are also necessary ingredients as marketplaces go global.

Product Search

While a good catalog should make it easier to find the desired product, a powerful search engine is an essential part of any large marketplace. Success of any good search function is to find and display exactly the detailed information the user is looking for.

Ordering

Once customers have found the desired product, clinching the deal depends on how easily they can place the order. Even a trace of friction can discourage the customer from taking the final step. Speeding up and implementing the automation plays a major role. The one-click ordering facility by Amazon is a classic example of how automation can help accelerate order placement. Collecting minimum information while providing maximum transparency and ensuring utmost security for payments are characteristics of a desirable ordering scheme. Preserving customer information, partnering with payment-processing systems for pre-approvals, and delighting the customer with surprise rebates and amazingly fast delivery plans can trigger the customer to confirm an order.

Life Cycle Management of KIA Assets

Most KIAs are time sensitive. Real-time streaming data, response time of AI models, duration of ads, and timing of a message or news are all obvious examples of the time-critical nature of KIA entities. The value of these entities diminishes with time. Collecting these KIA elements in a timely manner, processing them in real time, and making them available for consumption before they lose their significance is of paramount importance. Automation of every step of the life cycle is probably the only way to address this issue.

Updates

The transient nature of KIAs poses the additional challenge of making sure the assets are fresh and up to date. This is a situation different from other items in traditional marketplaces. Many of the KIA assets are like perishable commodities in that they need to be refreshed as time and context changes. Data tables need to be reloaded with the latest data, and models need to be updated as data changes. Without such updates, results can be wrong and unreliable. The frequency of updates and the triggers to update can be controlled properly only if the pipelines, valves, and meters of the KIA flow are automated. The problem becomes more prominent and critical as the size and diversity of these entities are scaled up. Moreover, the metadata of the KIA should include information such as the time of an update, the nature of the update, and what or who caused the update so that consumers can decide which version of the assets they should rely on. Also, this lineage info is essential for any postmortem analysis of event tracing, dependency tracking, debugging, and customer support.

Speed and Volume Issues

Many streaming data sources produce large volumes of data, such as satellite images, weather-tracking tools, even human-generated tweets and media uploads. This raises the issue of how fast the data can be processed and stored.

Ecosystem Around KIA Assets

Like traditional sales markets, online marketplaces also have certain essential services and some other desirable or viable services in addition to the main function of selling.

These include many different activities prior to sales, during the sales, and post-sales, such as price comparisons, product comparisons, and reviews.

Pricing and Price Comparisons

Pricing here doesn't just mean putting a price tag on an asset, but rather how pricing engines can optimally set prices, how to design and implement different pricing engines, and how to process rebates. Numerous pricing software packages are commercially available that automate pricing analytics, optimize prices, and execute pricing changes to help organizations make more-efficient and -effective pricing decisions. Players in this field are Vendavo[209], SAP[210], PROS[211], Feedvisor[212], PriceFx[213], Vistaar[214], and several others.

Payment Processing

Payment processing is closely associated with sales transactions. There are many ecosystem players, including credit card companies like Visa, Amex, Mastercard, PayPal, Google Pay, and other payment-processing companies.

Credit Services

In addition to depending on external payment services, many marketplaces offer their own credit cards (often partnered with Visa or Mastercard), similar to department-store credit cards. This becomes another service as part of the ecosystem.

Shipping

The shipping service that every marketplace needs to support was described earlier. In fact, this aspect of overall service is what makes digital marketplaces distinct from brick-and-mortar shops, where shipping services are optional or non-existent. Shipping partners or having one's own shipping and delivery service are essential for any online marketplace. Customer satisfaction begins at the purchase point and moves onward until the customer gets the purchased item in hand.

---

209 https://www.vendavo.com/glossary/pricing-software/

210 https://www.sap.com

211 https://pros.com/products/price-optimization-software/

212 https://feedvisor.com/feedvisor-360/

213 https://www.pricefx.com/

214 https://www.vistaar.com

Figure 7.1: Fallacy of Same Day Delivery

For KIA products, the situation is different. Almost all KIA products are delivered electronically, and in most cases the platforms themselves support goods delivery. Streaming and packaging services may employ third-party interfaces, tools, and communication channels.

The speed of delivery for KIA products is solely dependent on the bandwidth of the network and the volume or size of the assets delivered. The extra concern for electronic shipping is the security and reliability of the communication channels and ease of connection between the source and the destination.

Customer Support

Post-sales support for providing product clarifications, fixing defects, and helping the customer install and use the product are critical to the success of any marketplace and suppliers. Post-sales support is a necessary evil that often costs money and resources. The cost of sales needs to account for such support to improve customer satisfaction and achieve customer repeat business. Many suppliers, shops, and online markets outsource this function to other agencies that are specialized in dealing with customers.

Marketing

Online marketplaces also need marketing via conventional means (newspaper, TV, and internet ads), as well as electronic means (e-mail pushes and other social communication channels). Marketing functions are the same for both traditional and online marketplaces. An added advantage with online marketplaces is that sellers can employ more dynamic cross-selling and upselling techniques because they can track customer behavior via their portals.

Online trade shows, bidding websites, and auctions are much more scalable than other conventional means to promote a marketplace.

Product Reviews

Many marketplaces, as part of their catalogs, support product reviews by both subject-matter experts (SMEs) and real users who have already purchased the product. These feedback reviews act as good marketing tools. For the consumer, reviews are a great help in making the decision to buy the right product. Marketplace owners should aggregate product reviews sourced from buyers and product reviews solicited from SMEs to show overall ratings, as Amazon's five-star rating system does. The marketplace platform should support product review collection, aggregation, and publishing on a regular basis.

CHAPTER 8

NEGOTIATIONS

"One of the things I learned when I was negotiating was that until I changed myself,
I could not change others."
—Nelson Mandela

Negotiations are an integral part of any sales transaction. Buyer and seller
bargain over price and other contractual elements to make those terms meet their side's
specific advantage. This type of bargaining is prevalent in real estate, car purchasing,
farmers' markets, and many small-scale shop transactions. Online marketplaces started
with the famous example of Priceline. Although Priceline's business is centered around
offering only a "negotiated" price, many marketplaces may find it useful to support a
similar policy for an optional set of cataloged products.

Sometimes, buyer and seller may employ negotiation software to reach an
agreement that satisfies both parties. This type of software may help both sides
come up with a suitable agreement, as well as track the decision-making process.
Alternatively, negotiation software can function as a training program that teaches
negotiating skills. There are commercial tools and software available from third-
party suppliers to facilitate the sales negotiations. EEXAR[215], Zoho Contracts[216], and

215 https://www.eexar.com/eexar-negotiation/
216 https://www.zoho.com/contracts/negotiation.html

DocSend at Dropbox[217] are all examples of software tools for facilitating sales and contract negotiations.

Advertising

Supporting advertisements on the platform on products and services of third parties is a common practice on e-commerce platforms. This can also be a revenue-generation strategy. The marketplace may support ad engine services to self-onboard and self-support third-party ads to handle them at scale.

Co-selling and Upselling in KIA Marketplaces

Co-selling and upselling are common in all marketplaces. Electronic shops selling DVDs, cables, and fixtures often offer installation and maintenance services as well. Similarly, a data marketplace can offer consulting services for data management and analysis, hosting services for running data-related applications, and tools that provide data security, privacy protection, and analytics. Availability of SaaS-based or downloadable development tools are attractive components of an overall ecosystem.

Can KIA Marketplaces Include Conventional Physical Products?

Although KIA products are not physical entities, often their consumption requires physical devices and tools. For example, music is associated with headphones, speakers, and amplifiers. Image-recognition or processing software can be relevant components to associate with high-resolution cameras. A sophisticated AI model may require high-performance GPUs and other actuators as well. If there are closely related gadgets or components, based on the type of KIA entity involved, it may make sense to sell them as an offshoot of the main product sales on the same platform. Amazon and many marketplaces have successfully implemented this idea.

Recap

Scaling of marketplaces needs two main ingredients: a large collection of products to sell and a frictionless process to enable the sales. Both are aided by automation steps at every stage, and technology can play a big role in achieving desired growth. Success lies in making buying an enjoyable experience so that customers come back to the same platform again and again.

217 https://www.docsend.com/blog/improve-sales-negotiation-with-docsend/

CHAPTER 9

SOCIAL IMPACTS OF KIA MARKETPLACES

Introduction

Commerce is an integral part of society and culture that directly influences the economy, jobs, business growth, and personal relationships. Digitization of commerce has had huge impacts on all these factors, for good or ill. This chapter discusses how digital marketplaces have affected social life and societal frameworks.

Social Interactions

Obviously, the online marketplaces lack interpersonal interactions. Human interactions have multiple benefits, such as the ability to ask questions and get clarifications, the process of establishing a trust between the seller and buyer that often influences the deals, the ability to understand the emotions and reactions on both sides of a negotiation, the preferences of the customer, the potential to gauge the seller's eagerness and willingness to negotiate, and, most importantly, the opportunity to foster the process of person-to-person networking and relationship building. Although personal interactions are important to several types of product transactions, they likely have less effect on KIA product sales. This is primarily because sales of most KIA assets are technology products that rely on rigorous technical evaluation and experimentation rather than the product's look and feel or any other sentiments potential customers may have about the products or the marketplace's environment or personnel.

In the book titled *A Guide to Marketplaces*[218], the authors explain what types of marketplaces can thrive. The book observes that "monogamy"—those markets where buyers are fiercely loyal and use the same supplier every time—reduces a marketplace's value. For example, once consumers find a doctor or cleaning service they like and trust, it's easier for the consumers to stick with the known provider rather than take a chance on, or spend time searching for, someone new. This means there's little need for the consumer to use the marketplace again. The same dynamic is also true with commoditized products where the marketplace sources products from the same supplier. Social interactions are mostly affected by such monogamous marketplaces.

Crowd opinion is a key social influence. When the parking lot of a shop is full or the checkout lines are long, those factors often have a positive marketing impact on potential customers. Of course, these examples may also have minor negative impacts; customers may perceive wait times as being longer or become discouraged due to lack of adequate parking spaces. In online marketplaces, the wait times and car parking or travel inhibitors are irrelevant.

Personal experiences and social aspects that are missing in online marketplaces include the exposure to shops or a mall and the associated physical proximity that allows for seeing and touching the products, the opportunity for customers to notice items other than those they were intending to buy, and shopping with family and friends. However, the impact may be less on customers who don't have as much nostalgia about roaming around shopping malls and doing window shopping (such as Gen Y shoppers, who are accustomed to shopping online).

Democratization of Asset Building, Ownership, and Trading

The ease with which assets can be cataloged, onboarded, and sold through the digital marketplaces is a two-sided coin, as we'll see in the rest of this chapter. It opens the trading platform to any type of suppliers from (mostly) anywhere in the world, especially important when the assets are KIA products.

Online marketplaces provide an even playing field for small and big-scale suppliers and manufacturers. Some of the advantages are as follows:

- Minimum infrastructure expenses—A marketplace doesn't need expensive infrastructure to start selling. Most marketplace platforms facilitate easy onboarding with no upfront fees and a limited validation or vetting process. Literally, owners can start selling assets in hours.

218 https://versionone.vc/marketplaces-guide-ed3/

- Built-in marketing and promotion—These aspects are automatically taken care of by traffic on the marketplace platform, search mechanisms, and personalized catalogs.

- Wider audience—Online marketplaces offer massive customer exposure that crosses boundaries of towns, countries, time zones, and continents by being open around the clock.

These factors have significant social and economic impacts, such as avoidance of middlemen who may cut into profits, faster source-to-market transition, and quicker turnaround for investments. This gives lots of power to small players and those who don't have the business expertise of larger competitors.

Economic Impacts

Digital marketplaces have grown in size, volume of transactions for goods, and revenue flow.

There are a number of invisible economic impacts too. The growth impact of the goods-delivery industry triggered by online trade is one example that is interesting to observe. The number of UPS delivery trucks has grown tremendously because of the need to deliver online-ordered goods to customers' premises. Amazon is experimenting with the delivery of goods via the age-old network of U.S. post offices. Sunday delivery and late-evening deliveries have become a norm in the shipping industry. This has resulted in positive changes in the bottom-line financials of major shipping companies like UPS, FedEx, and a host of local delivery agencies.

The ability to change prices and execute "flash sales" is another natural phenomenon created by online marketplaces. There are service companies that dynamically scavenge the online marketplaces hour by hour and provide alerts on new sale prices, price comparisons, and best deals. The instantaneous response to market demands, inventory levels, and socio-economic events makes online marketplaces vibrant and mutually beneficial to both suppliers and consumers.

Ease of Transactions

One of the good impacts of digital marketplaces is that they have made transactions much easier and quicker. Transactions at online marketplaces need no waiting at the checkout stations, avoid crowding aisles with popular goods, and eliminate the need to carry the goods home.

The 24x7 availability of digital purchases is obviously another big plus point. A bigger advantage is the anonymity of purchases. Digital marketplaces facilitate buying and selling anonymously, especially any goods that are personally sensitive.

However, anonymous buying has some dangerous aspects, such as enabling purchase of unauthorized items by ineligible people. Marketplaces need to establish checks on the authenticity of the buyers.

Diversity of Choices

Amazon and Alibaba are clear examples of the power of product diversity. Both act as huge supermarkets offering products from paper clips to large furniture and equipment, from small software applications to cloud platform services. Digital marketplaces have an inherent capability to grow instantaneously given technology-driven automation. This provides opportunity for all stakeholders:

- Consumers get to shop for all types of goods at one place with one account.
- Producers can find an "aisle or shelf" for their assets irrespective of the type of product, quantity at hand to sell, or price levels.
- Cross-sellers and ad agencies have a wide range of choices for targeted marketing and sales campaigns.

One-stop shopping has affected shopping patterns, as evident from the shift of crowd buying habits from Black Friday (brick-and-mortar) to Cyber Monday (online).

Jobs

Retail has long been a major employment sector influencing the economy and social structure around it. Digital marketplaces have had a transformative impact on retail sales jobs. With the growth of digital marketplaces, the types of jobs also have changed. There is less need for brick-and-mortar shops. Those jobs have shifted to large-warehouse workers who arrange and pack goods (sales order execution). Checkout clerks' positions are being eliminated, and customer service representatives are less in demand. On the support side, there are more tech workers who develop and maintain online cataloging systems, checkout systems, and payment systems. More content-developer positions are required. An army of data scientists and business analytics personnel are needed to sift through the data to generate valuable insights with which to optimize online platform operations. This shift from traditional shop-floor jobs to more tech-centric jobs has caused major disruptions, both socially and financially. The shift from blue-collar jobs to college-educated, white-collar jobs is always painful to any societal fabric, and it will take time to smooth out the kinks caused by these changes before full acceptance can be realized.

New Economies

Digital marketplaces and the ability to digitize almost everything have resulted in new ways to build and enhance the economy. The best examples are commodities and items that previously were not identified as assets, but which are now easier to monetize. Unused rooms in a home, rarely used equipment and appliances, ridesharing, homemade food, and handmade arts and crafts have now found huge value in terms of sharing and monetization. This has created new economically viable markets and created jobs and income for many. Uber and Airbnb stirred and stimulated the economy by digitally connecting suppliers and consumers. The ability to reach out to consumers in any corner of the world has scaled up sales and spurred the economy in a way that's never previously happened in such a short span of time.

Virtually all marketplaces create efficiency. They make it easier for buyers and sellers to find each other and complete a transaction. But not all marketplaces create value equally. For example, marketplaces may connect schools with substitute teachers, visiting doctors with hospitals, and commercial landlords with retailers interested in creating pop-up shops. These all certainly increase efficiency, but they might not necessarily expand the market. The likely reason is because there is finite supply and demand. In other words, a new marketplace won't create a new crop of teachers, doctors, schools, or hospitals. In the absence of an online marketplace, both sides would probably find each other eventually but maybe in a less efficient way.

The best marketplaces can tap into new groups of participants and increase the overall number of transactions. The sharing economy is a great example of creating value. People who never thought they'd be landlords or hotel proprietors are now hosts on Airbnb. People who never thought they'd transport people for money are now drivers for Uber. These platforms empower whole new groups of people to become sellers.

Recap

Just like any technology transformation, online trading also has significant influences on social fabric and behaviors. There are many examples of major brick-and-mortar shops and malls becoming local landmarks, stimulating a local economy by creating ancillary shops and businesses and even influencing the art and culture of the surroundings. Examples include Macy's in New York, the Mall of America in Minneapolis, and festivals in major marketplace locations. Such influences and contributions become absent when trading goes online. The experience of meeting friends and neighbors at the shopping places and the process of retailers generating ancillary local employment have been adversely affected by the advent of digital trading.

CHAPTER 10

KIA MARKETPLACES: BUILDING IT RIGHT, CHALLENGES BEYOND THE BUSINESS AND TECHNOLOGY

"We cannot solve our problems with the same thinking we used when we
created them."
—Albert Einstein

Introduction

While the biggest opportunity for digital marketplaces is the worldwide stakeholders,
the marketplace's global nature itself offers some challenges. These include localization
(language, metrics, and currency) considerations, in addition to the issues of delivering
goods across continents. The nature of KIA products alleviates these issues to a great
extent because the delivery can mostly be done by electronic means. For example, data,
software, photos, and models can be transferred to buyers via digital networks. Cloud-
based streaming services can handle entertainment products, courseware, and ads.
When transactions happen across borders, there are concerns about pricing policies,
tax considerations, and local legal restrictions. For example, the definition of a valid
transaction can be different in different countries. Language and cultural issues have a
strong influence on courseware, ads, music, and videos. The following sections of this
chapter cover these topics.

The cross-border e-commerce market is expected to grow as advanced technologies
help reduce issues with international payments, long shipping times, and language
barriers, making it possible to shop online anywhere and everywhere. The compound

annual growth rate (CAGR) is projected to be more than 15 percent, to reach more than $5 trillion[219] in market potential. While impressive, there are certainly challenges regarding payments, shipping, tracking, returns, customs procedures, and international taxation patterns[220] that still need to be resolved.

Payments

Pricing in different currencies and payment in the local currencies are major hurdles. The prices should reflect the local economy, as competition may require more than just conversion of currency exchanges. It becomes further complicated because currency rates are dynamic, and the fluctuations can impact profits.

Payment processing is a complex process because different countries have their own particular arrangements and restrictions for processing digital payments. In some countries, cash payment on delivery of goods requires local agencies to collect payments and make subsequent remittances to platform owners or suppliers.

Shipping and Tracking of Delivery

Delivery of goods is probably the hardest part of international commerce. Shipping across country borders takes more time and is more expensive than shipping within the country where the goods reside. Local warehouses and local sourcing are potential solutions. However, there are goods that are manufactured only in specific locations, which necessitates physical shipping of goods to the end consumer. When the delivery is over long distances (which is time-consuming), tracking of the goods becomes more important. Although shipping across borders may require changing hands between different companies, thus making tracking even more difficult, it's heartening to note that major shipping companies like FedEx and UPS have international operations that make it easier to track the shipping status of any asset.

Shipping is less of a problem when it comes to KIA products because in most cases they are already in digital format and can be sent across the internet to global destinations. However, as applicable for any electronic transactions, infringement and hacking affecting the integrity and safety of the contents are a constant concern. Because different countries may have widely varying regulations, cross-border security management can be a nightmare. Moreover, there are added inspections, restrictions

---

219 https://www.polarismarketresearch.com/industry-analysis/cross-border-b2c-e-commerce-market

220 https://gepard.io/ecommerce-strategy/cross-border-ecommerce

mposed by export controls, and privacy regulations that make cross-border transfers a
cumbersome process.

Returns

If the shipping is complicated, handling the returns is even more challenging. For KIA
products, the return is often a license-reversion process in which there's little control
over unauthorized replication of an asset that's been sold but returned after customer
acceptance. No wear-and-tear inspections or misuse of KIA assets are possible. This
may inspire use of "no-return" policies for some critical categories of KIA assets.

Customs and Export-Restricting Regulations

Each country has its own unique product restrictions that affect international commerce.
The local government, or sometimes international bodies, lay out these restrictive
measures. Some of the cross-border e-commerce examples of restricted products
include medication, food, defense-related technologies, and, most prominently, KIA
products like photographs, videos, models, cryptography algorithms, certain software
source code, and personal and governmental data and its derivatives. The restrictions
on KIA products are dynamic and are based on time, who produces them, who owns
them, and who uses them.

Taxation

Tax policies, structures, and rates widely vary across the globe, which is a major hurdle
for cross-border commerce. Determining the right tax structure, collecting the taxes
at the right time of sales, and making appropriate payments to multiple governmental
agencies are major pain points that need their own governing establishment within
any platform company. Avoiding double taxation is equally as important as collecting
and remitting the right tax for different types of goods. The point of sale (city, county,
state, and country) and the time of sale are crucial for accurate tax computation. The
process becomes more complicated because the price structure may vary from country
to country.

Language and Locale Restrictions

Support for local language, metrics, and currency is necessary to enable international
trade. The foot-pound-second (FPS) system is followed by the U.S., and some other
countries may not be familiar with the meter-kilogram-second (MKS) system used
by many European and Asian countries. Power voltage and frequency is another

specification issue for all powered gadgets. Language and cultural variations also need to be supported for both physical and virtual objects. Specifications should reflect local preferences with simple examples like mileage per gallon of gas versus mileage per liter of petrol. This lack of international standards becomes more predominant when it comes to KIA assets, because the data, models, ads, educational styles, and photos need to cater to the local interests of the different global markets being addressed. An ad relating to Thanksgiving or Halloween may not be relevant in Asian countries, for example. Although globalization and effective communication channels have made the world more flat, customers' expectations are often tied to their social and cultural roots.

Cultural Impact

Digital commerce through online marketplaces has a significant impact on the social fabric of commerce itself. Consider the fact that, with online shopping, participants can buy and sell almost anything anytime anywhere. Marketplaces that operate 24x7 help in multiple ways. Shoppers can place an order any time of day or night from the comfort of their homes, from their workplaces, at airports, from movie theaters, or while traveling. This has two impacts: first, the ease and convenience of "shop on demand" is recognized, and second, because there's no need to defer a purchase until the next day when shops are open, there's often a tendency to order more goods than necessary. For sellers, the availability of remote markets and the ease of cataloging goods without almost any investment makes it much easier to monetize assets that are new, used, archived, or even thrown into garbage bins. This makes it possible to add monetary value to goods otherwise considered not worthy of selling.

Traditionally, shopping is not about buying things alone. It's often a joint activity with friends or other family members. Families enjoy going out to shop with children, who enjoy looking at things and doing window shopping. The group activity of shopping is practically absent in online commerce. There is a distinct possibility that virtual shopping together will become a reality with advances in metaverse-based applications. Until then, the social experience of shopping—meeting one's neighbors, colleagues, and friends at shopping malls; and eating or playing while shopping—will remain absent in online shopping. Although the busy roads and the lines at the checkout stations are not a desirable aspect of physical shopping, the experiences (good and bad) will be missing and will have a profound effect on the process, structure, and psychology of shopping. Many cultures evolved around trading, and associated human experiences will be missed in current digital marketplaces.

Restrictions on Types of Consumption and Usage

The way goods are consumed has a great impact on the way they are delivered or shipped. KIA assets stand apart in the sense that purchased assets need to be delivered in an appropriate format—almost all the time electronically—even though sometimes the ownership is changed or only shared in cases where the assets remain in place (similar to real estate). The sections below cover some specific features of KIA delivery, consumption, and usage.

Downloadable

Self-shopping is probably the most desirable form of sales transactions, whether it's via traditional shops or an online marketplace. Consumers directly pick up what they want or to which they are entitled. There's no need for additional assistance. For KIA assets, this entails direct downloading of the goods from the marketplace platform or another source portal. All the asset providers must assure is that the contents are downloadable in some standard format or package, such as Comma Separated Values (CSVs), an executable, or JSON files. Ownership is transferred once the download takes place and the sales transaction is completed. The platform owner or asset provider should make sure that the published service-level agreements (SLAs) are maintained for facilitating the download without affecting integrity of the contents and in an acceptable transfer time.

Streaming

Many KIA products are generated and consumed in real time. The fundamental notion is that continuously generated data needs to be collected and consumed in real time. In most cases, the value will be diminished or lost if the data is not delivered and consumed on time.

The platform or the asset provider needs to offer a streaming interface that delivers the purchased asset. Streaming assets also have a dependency on the consumer side, so the consumer platform or interface should be able to accept the streaming information and process it in time. These subscription services will often have a dedicated wired or wireless connection already established between the source and destination.

Shared

Shared consumption is another form of transaction in which the asset is shared across multiple consumers. The assets are housed in a central place and either access is provided to multiple consumers or a copy is provided to different users.

Asset as a Service (AaaS)

AaaS is an extension of the shared items business model. Typically, data, software, models, and digital twins are hosted in the cloud and consumers access them as a service—bringing in their input data and collecting the results—as needed. The shared box and online office tools are typical examples of an AaaS type of consumption.

Liability Considerations

Liability coverage on items that are sold on a platform is no different from that of conventional brick-and-mortar shops and digital marketplaces. However, the KIA products are often not sold (except for audio and video media and some software) in traditional shops, so sellers have some additional liability considerations. Lineage has also become a concern in traditional physical goods, covering factors such as whether the workers were paid adequately, from which country the asset originated, and possible environmental impacts. There are extreme precautions for food items, drugs, toys, and cosmetics with all types of fine print to protect the suppliers and sales agencies from any adverse legal actions. Data, models, software, courseware, and similar products have added issues related to privacy, bias, resource consumption, and legality certifications, which often create new types of issues for those who create the goods and those who facilitate their sales. The correctness and truth of many KIA asset types are often subjective, regardless of acceptance of their trading and monetization.

Vendor Certification

In an open marketplace platform, there can be many suppliers of products of different types and brands, levels of quality, price points, origin locations, and sizes and scales. Although the primary responsibility for acceptance of the products lies with the suppliers or owners of the assets, the marketplace owners also share some responsibility because the transactions happen via their platforms. Selecting the right vendors or vetting the vendors thoroughly is critical to the success of the platform. A trusted, popular, or famous vendor always brings in added trust, increases traffic, and attracts other similar vendors. The opposite is also true; one bad vendor and the associated bad experience can have a severe adverse impact on a platform's reputation.

Each platform needs to establish its guiding principles, criteria, and process for vendor qualification. These may be specific to the product type, industry rules, consumer demands, and government rules and regulations.

Vendor certification is an important component of a total quality-management system that assures that a supplier's product is produced, packaged, and shipped under a controlled process that results in consistent conformance to customer requirements. The primary objective of the certification process is to assure consistent high quality as demonstrated by predictable conformance to a marketplace's requirements. The vendor approval may have several steps, such as establishing the certification criteria. These criteria include the minimum requirements, tests, evaluation steps, documents and other evidence to be submitted, specifying an expert group that will be evaluating the vendor, documenting test results, assessing the level of certification achieved, the process and frequency of recertification, the product inspection process, and guaranteeing the published quality standards.

Ethical Considerations

The basic principle of any market is that as long as there's a consumer and a supplier available, trading can happen. However, there are boundaries, just like in any other scenario. A responsible platform shouldn't allow any transactions or operations that are potentially damaging to the people, society, or environment. The credibility of the marketplace will improve if the business can consider social consciousness over quick profits. Each platform needs to consider what items it is selling, who the suppliers are, how the items are acquired or produced, how they are priced, who is buying them, and how the buyer is using the purchased item. An example is the responsible decision made by IBM not to sell face-recognition software because of the concern that it could be used for illegal and unethical applications, such as tracking and profiling people.

KIA products are much more susceptible to unethical usage being created via unethical processes. Dark data, AI models that are built with biased data, ads that misrepresent the facts, courseware that teaches how to build dangerous or harmful products such as bombs, photos that depict people or objects incorrectly or in unacceptable standards—all of these are common examples of unethical practices. Freedom of expression and action are favored; however, primary consideration should be the safety and comfort of the general audience rather than the rights of one individual or group. Each marketplace platform needs to design, publish, and enforce the ethical principles it intends to stand by.

Recap

Establishing and operating a marketplace goes beyond stacking or cataloging products and enabling payments. The end-to-end experience of buying and selling involves several factors that need attention, such as personalization, transparency of product specifications, visibility of the process, and quickness of delivery. The success of

Amazon Marketplace is due to the ease of buying, the wide range of products, and the huge number of vendors it provides. It's not easy to achieve marketplace success; however, there are important functions and best practices that need to be learned about marketplaces. There are also other measures of success, such as the ease with which one can share photos with Google Photos, the convenience of getting an Uber ride, the ability to sell one's handicrafts on Facebook Marketplace, and the extensive list of items one can find on eBay. All these point to how digitization can benefit all of us in the business of trade and enhance the experience of buying and selling.

CHAPTER 11

KIA MARKETPLACES: TRENDS AND FUTURE DIRECTIONS

"The most reliable way to predict the future is to create it."
—Abraham Lincoln

Introduction

With the extensive investigations conducted and observations made on KIA marketplaces, it is fair to make some projections about their future trends and directions. The future scenario looks bright but not without noting some cautions and concerns. It is important to cite some significant landmarks, express a few emerging concerns that are likely shared by many, and try to paint what the KIA marketplace may look like in the coming years.

What Are Successful Use Case Scenarios?

The past decade witnessed the proliferation and maturation of online marketplaces. With the widespread adoption of smartphones, the reach of these marketplaces has grown to masses that include people who are not technology savvy. Marketplaces extended from products to services and then to crowd-sourcing. Examples are Uber, Lyft[221], TaskRabbit, Indeed, Adobe[222], Facebook (Meta), and TikTok[223]. The pandemic period of 2020 through 2022 further accelerated the ordering and delivery of services in almost all sectors. Tesla, for instance, has been successful in selling cars without opening a sales office or having many salespeople. The authors remember similar experiments two decades ago, like CarOrder.com, which failed miserably because it was ahead of its time. Consumers were not ready, and technology could not support it effectively. KIA marketplaces benefit from the two decades of lessons learned and the best practices established by marketplaces selling physical goods.

What Are the Ethical Considerations?

There are always strong concerns about any transformation, whether it's societal, cultural, technological, financial, political, or religious. Some of the often-asked questions are covered in the following paragraphs.

Can personalization lead to limiting the information that the user is exposed to?

Personalization enables people to see and access opportunities based on their interests, which makes marketplace usage more efficient. However, personalization has the side effect that the user, once profiled a certain way, may not get exposure to other diverse products or experiences due to being in a filter bubble. This can have some negative impacts. For example, if a person is profiled as politically inclined in one direction, based on past or current actions, that person may get fewer chances to view diverse opinions and trends. This can be especially dangerous in early childhood, when markets could bias society strongly in a particular way. A classic example is the influence of the meme "pizza is the favorite of many children" going on to influence food preferences of whole generations. Not only early introduction and branding caused this effect, but peer influence may also have been a factor here.

221 https://www.lyft.com
222 https://www.adobe.com/
223 https://www.tiktok.com/en/

Too much personalization can prevent free information flow. Users may not know what other options are available, some of which could be better for them rather than those dictated by the algorithms. The algorithms, although powerful and based on historical data, can overlook the diverse interests the user may have and often underestimate the creativity and ambition inherent in all human beings. We need to be mindful to ensure that the users are not unduly influenced by a filter bubble, which could limit exposing a broader set of KIA products across the globe.

Is there too much information collected about the users, leading to risks to personal safety and bias?

Figure 10.1: Data and Privacy

Encroachment of personalization into personal privacy has become an increasingly concerning trend. Availability of personal data through social media, online purchases, personal e-mail communications, blogs, association memberships, and clubs pours a lot more data into external hands and media. These seemingly disparate sources are often harvested by clever marketers employing powerful algorithms to make recommendations and display targeted ads. The above cartoon[224] showing the levels of

---

224 www.marketoonist.com

this influence is clear about the boundaries of this personalization approach. Under the pretexts of freeware, free subscriptions, cash back, and other privileges, businesses and socio-political establishments collect a lot more data than the average person may want to share—and often more than collectors need. Unless this information is adequately protected and used only for appropriate objectives, it could be harmful to life, society, and the economy. Marketplace owners need to be mindful that KIA products do not impinge on the privacy of consumers and that consumer security is paramount.

Do digital platforms pave the way for faster scaling and potential monopoly?

Because physical space is not needed for expanding the number of wares that are sold in a physical store and that local logistics can support—such as permission from local authorities, parking space, billboards, and employees to manage the store—are irrelevant, digital marketplaces can grow and scale up relatively easily. The time to grow to massive scale is relatively short if automation tools are available to vet the vendors, onboard item catalogs, and automate the marketing campaigns. Furthermore, the "success breeds success" factor aids today's exponential growth of digital marketplaces. The number of concurrent shoppers can be theoretically unlimited if the platform infrastructure (computing and storage) can support that, which is easier than building large physical malls.

The easy path to massive scaling in a short time, especially for KIA products, can also lead to potential monopolies. Digital marketplaces optimize the cost of selling with the help of on-demand selling, in-time shipping with minimal warehouse inventory, and absence of human agents at the storefronts. Such efficiencies could lead to better prices and, coupled with large catalogs, raise the possibility that digital marketplaces will come to dominate and even displace other smaller players.

Some of these consequences are simply part of a digital transformation. Modern days have seen the examples of the complete disappearance of video rental stores—for example, the Blockbuster chain store—due to online competition. Amazon quickly led to the demise of many brick-and-mortar bookshops and other online booksellers as well. However, to be fair, the very fact that online marketplaces can quickly grow to dominate a market space also facilitates bold new players to come in. Netflix seems to be losing some of its steam even as Amazon Prime TV, Hulu, and similar streaming services are emerging strongly. Traditional trading houses like Walmart made a strong impact on online markets and gave Amazon good competition.

Specialty marketplaces focus on specific categories of products to attract more buyers who are living in their own focused worlds. Although there are easier ways of establishing monopolies, virtual marketplaces are a level playing field for anyone with the right business acumen and advanced technology. Optimizing the cost of selling, ease of finding and buying items, and level of customer service are the only deciding factors—and not just for online marketplaces. All marketplaces characterized by these values can be expected to give better service and price advantages to consumers.

Can fake platforms emerge for making quick profits before disappearing?

One of the concerns of consumers and suppliers is the stability of online marketplaces. Because face-to-face, personal interactions (during which buyers and sellers actually meet) are mostly absent, long-term reliability of marketplaces remaining in business is often a question. The ease and speed with which online markets can pop into existence points to the fact that they may disappear just as quickly, leaving both suppliers and consumers high and dry. This is different from physical shops, where one can see signs of impending changes or even go to the location and find out what is happening. One must verify the authenticity and stability of new marketplaces, not only because they can potentially endanger the validity and execution of past transactions, but more to understand the risks of providing personal and financial information such as address, phone numbers, and credit card information. Just as in any field, foul players are a norm rather than the exception, so it's imperative for all stakeholders to take extra caution.

Many governments and other trade agencies have started establishing rules and regulations for proper and safe functioning of online trade. The EU's "One Stop Shop" acts[225] are one example. These cover tax-related rules, value-added taxing, marketplace definitions, and trade distances and their impacts. In the U.S., the Federal Trade Commission (FTC) has the responsibility of enforcing the policies and rules regarding trade, including e-commerce. The document "International Consumer Protection and Cooperation" published by the FTC[226] throws some light on prevailing regulations.

How do we ensure the quality of goods with online purchases?

The authenticity and lineage of KIA assets need to be verified and published to make them trustworthy and acceptable. In fact, this isn't an issue specific to digital

225 https://vat-one-stop-shop.ec.europa.eu/index_en
226 https://www.ftc.gov/policy/international/international-consumer-protection-cooperation

marketplaces. The very nature of KIA assets makes it difficult to verify their quality and reliability. There have been some attempts recently to set common standards and certifications for quality and reliability of data and AI products; however, the variety and nature of applications, such as data analytics and models—and the creative nature of some KIA assets like music, videos, and ads—make it difficult to establish any common yardsticks and measurement strategies for KIA asset quality and reliability. The type and name of the suppliers and the opinions of other users are probably the most dependable trust factors. Documenting asset lineage should also shed some light. In most cases, the supplier should offer sample assets or a brief time for experimentation to establish asset trust and credibility before expecting the consumer to make a final decision.

What Are the Trends?

Deep cognitive functions and even intellectual works could become digitally producible with the advances made in generative AI, which may further increase the volume of knowledge-intensive products and services. Examples like offering legal consulting, preparing business letters, building resumes, generating reports, developing custom software code, tutoring, and even giving medical advice could be available as new "intelligent services," given the current capabilities of foundation models and generative-AI techniques. The importance of these types of services is that they are probably the most highly valued services, ones currently offered only by human domain experts who are well trained and experienced in their own disciplines.

The emerging business models in this space look promising, but at the same time, they are concerns from the point of view of reliability and the disruptive effects of these services. In particular, the impact of the emerging availability and potential proliferation of these services may diminish the need for "finished products" such as APIs, models, and data. For example, data could be synthetically generated or real data can be supplied by intelligent agencies. Software code can be created on demand. It wouldn't be surprising if eventually such "Uber-like" services, powered by foundational models, could adversely impact the sale of products in the coming years— just like availability of Uber ride sharing has discouraged people from owning vehicles.

With the advent of more immersive interfaces like the metaverse, increased automation, ease of use, and accuracy can be realizable in remote diagnostics, remote inspection, remote instruction, and remote government services.

Marketplace breakthroughs have yet to arrive in a significant manner in the health care sector. Online "hiring" of doctors, online counseling, online senior care, and online delivery of medicines have yet to become widely accepted, not because there are no technology enablers, but because losing the social expectations of meeting and talking to a doctor in person are slowing it down and because the insurance industry is hesitant to modernize its processes and practices.

Another area that can dramatically change will be tourism and sports, which still require physical travel and personal presence. Imagine the archeological museums, memorial buildings and structures, and scenic locations that could be experienced remotely with the advent of 3D simulation and augmented reality (AR), which could save time and money for tourists and be especially beneficial for the handicapped or elderly. Near-real-life experiences, if provided for sports and games events, would let users enjoy the events while sitting in the comfort of their homes. The AR and virtual reality (VR) worlds can hopefully provide realistic context with cheering friends in the gallery—and perhaps including soda and popcorn dispensers.

Widespread adoption of digital wallets for payments would be another big transformation arena supporting the growth of e-commerce. More secure and convenient digital non-cash payment schemes will accelerate online trading.

Distributed sourcing across the globe and innovations in delivery schemes are other support functions that will fuel online trading. Today, the purchase transaction can happen in seconds; however, order realization is still the rub, although progress is being made in this area. Novel schemes of item delivery can lead to not only true 24x7 shopping but also on-demand shopping. In the long run, advances in delivery can lead to a habitual change in shopping patterns as people buy only the items they need right now, adding a market enlivened by more dynamism of daily and seasonal product mixes and prices.

Recap

The future is anybody's imagination. Automation, infusion of AI, optimization, and user-friendliness are the keys to the success of modern digital marketplace platforms. The possibilities are unlimited. With KIA products, virtual consumption and *in situ* usage of acquired assets offer opportunities that didn't exist even five years ago. This doesn't mean human-to-human interactions won't be needed; however, they could be on a different plane. Digital tools offer better ways of understanding the consumer and the seller and do a much better job of matching the suppliers and buyers, as well as unlocking additional efficiency and the prospect of better-quality goods and services at an optimal price level.

Creative minds blended with rapid advances in technology can lead to new marketplaces and marketable goods. Exciting times are ahead. It seems only appropriate to end this book with the following thoughtful quote.

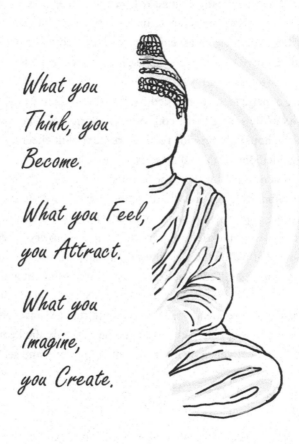

What you
Think, you
Become.

What you Feel,
you Attract.

What you
Imagine,
you Create.

Term	Description
Adversarial Robustness	Adversarial robustness refers to a model's ability to resist being fooled.
Computer-Aided Design (CAD)	CAD is a general-purpose term representing all types of automation software to simulate and generate engineering drawings and artifacts, which includes integrated circuit designs, aircraft engine simulations, computational fluid dynamics, and similar applications.
Comma Separated Values (CSV) Format	A CSV file is a plain-text file that stores data by delimiting data entries with commas. CSV files are often used when data needs to be compatible with many different programs.
Dark Data	Dark data is a general notion for any information assets organizations collect, process, and store during regular business activities but generally fail to use for other purposes, or information assets that are unusable because of reasons such as incompleteness, inconsistent formats, bias, and inappropriate contents.
Data Lineage	Lineage of data includes detailed information on the "history" of data from its origination to the present date. These may include the source, the way it was created, the ownership, the transformations that have happened to it, and the transformations' sequence. Sometimes it can be part of the metadata that is associated with data and should be updated in a timely fashion. Data lineage includes the data origin, what happens to it, and where it moves over time. These may include rich information on how the data was captured and processed, who are the people involved, who were the owners, and any information that relates to a stage or event in its life cycle.
Digital Twins	Digital Twins are computer software representations of the structure and behavior of corresponding physical entities. Typical examples are models that represent automobile engines, aircraft designs, wind tunnels, large machinery, human body organs, buildings, and similarly complex physical systems.

Term	Description
Foundation Model	A foundation model is an AI neural network—trained on mountains of raw data, generally with unsupervised learning—that can be adapted to accomplish a broad range of tasks. Examples are GPT-3, GPT-4 from Open AI, and PaLM from Google.
Graphics Processing Units (GPUs)	GPUs are synonymous with high-performance processors earlier employed in computationally intensive graphics processing and complex mathematical computations. In today's world, GPUs are mostly employed in large machine-learning model development requiring enormous computing power, such as AI applications.
Homomorphic Encryption	Homomorphic encryption is a form of encryption that enables computations to be performed on encrypted data without first having to decrypt it. The resulting computations are left in an encrypted form, which, when decrypted, results in an output that is identical to that produced had the operations been performed on the unencrypted data. Homomorphic encryption can be used for privacy-preserving outsourced storage and computation. This enables data to be encrypted and outsourced to commercial cloud environments for processing.
JavaScript Object Notation (JSON)	JSON is an open standard file- and data-interchange format that uses human-readable text to store and transmit data objects consisting of attribute-value pairs and arrays. It's a common data format with diverse uses in electronic data interchange, including that of web applications with servers.
K-12	K-12 is typical notation used in USA to indicate kindergarten to 12th grade in schools.
Knowledge Intensive Assets (KIAs)	KIAs are assets, products, and any cognitive entities that emerge from knowledge or aid in creating, developing, and managing knowledge.
Key Performance Indicators (KPIs)	KPIs are the critical (key) quantifiable indicators of progress toward an intended result. KPIs provide a focus for strategic and operational improvement, create an analytical basis for decision-making, and help focus attention on what matters most.
Model Drift	Model drift is the decay of a model's predictive power because of the changes in real-world environments. These may include the changes in statistical properties of dependent or independent variables that affect a model's predictive power.
Model Evasion	Model evasion refers to designing an input that seems normal for a human but is wrongly classified by machine-learning (ML) models. A typical example is to change some pixels in a picture before uploading so that the image-recognition system fails to classify the result.

Term	Description
Model Poisoning	Model poisoning refers to the malicious act of providing wrong or corrupted data for model training. One of the most pertinent threats to AI systems is the potential for their training data to be poisoned.
Model Theft	Model theft is an attack in the machine-learning settings when an adversary aims to obtain a copy model through querying the target model. This is a type of attack on AI models (especially Machine Learning as a Service, or MLaaS, models) causing responses from a victim model regarding queries made by an adversary.
Net Promoter Score (NPS)	NPS is a widely used market research metric that is based on a single survey question asking respondents to rate the likelihood that they would recommend a company, product, person, or service.
Near-Field Communication (NFC)	NFC is a set of short-range wireless technologies, typically requiring 4cm or less to initiate a connection. An example of NFC is a contactless payment system, such as Apple Pay or Google Pay.
Non-Fungible Token (NFT)	Non-fungible means something that is unique and can't be replaced. By contrast, physical money and cryptocurrencies are fungible, which means they can be traded or exchanged for one another.
Production Platform	Production platform refers to the system (on-premises or cloud-based) where software is run for regular use.
Release Platform	Release platform refers to a repository or storage media where production-ready software is available to download or deploy.
Single-Table and Multi-Table Data	These terms refer to representation of data where each of the records or rows will have identical structure and semantics. This is the most common and traditional way data is represented, especially for machine processing. Single-table entails all data in a single table and is typical for simple databases and data warehouses. Multi-table databases represent data organized in multiple related tables in which the tables are linked using fields called keys.
Service-Level Agreements (SLAs)	An SLA sets the expectations between the service provider and the customer and describes the products or services to be delivered, the single point of contact for end-user problems, and the metrics by which the effectiveness of the process will be monitored and approved.

Term	Description
Timeseries Data	This subgroup of data has a connotation that the data contents are time-related, such as daily or monthly information or real-time data generated by transactions or devices with a time stamp.
Uncertainty Quantification (UQ)	UQ is the science of quantitative characterization and estimation of uncertainties in both computational and real-world applications. It tries to determine how likely certain outcomes are if some aspects of the system are not exactly known. Weather prediction, disease prognosis, and the impact of certain economic events are all good examples.
Zero Trust	Zero trust is a security model or principle that is based on the notion "never trust, always verify," which means that devices should not be trusted by default, even if they are connected to a permissioned network such as a corporate LAN and even if they were previously verified.

BIBLIOGRAPHY

1. John McMillan, *Reinventing the Bazaar*, W. W. Norton & Company, https://wwnorton.com/

2. "Ecommerce Statistics: Industry benchmarks & growth," https://www.insiderintelligence.com/insights/ecommerce-industry-statistics/

3. James Risley, "What are the top online marketplaces?," Digital Commerce 360, https://www.digitalcommerce360.com/article/infographic-top-online-marketplaces/

4. "Value of Data: The Dawn of Data Marketplaces," Accenture – Western Digital Report, https://www.accenture.com/us-en/insights/high-tech/dawn-of-data-marketplace

5. "Coronavirus: US oil has dropped to below $0 dollars a barrel. Here's what it means," World Economic Forum, April 2020, https://www.weforum.org/agenda/2020/04/oil-barrel-prices-economic-supply-demand-coronavirus-covid19-united-states/

6. Marketplace: Wikipedia, https://en.wikipedia.org/wiki/Marketplace

7. Clifford Maxwell and Scott Duke Kominers, "What Makes an Online Marketplace Disruptive?," Harward Business Review, May 2021, https://hbr.org/2021/05/what-makes-an-online-marketplace-disruptive

8. Uber: "Tech Company to help make movement happen" https://www.uber.com

9. Priceline: Travel Innovator, https://www.priceline.com

10. Airbnb: https://www.airbnb.com

11. Substack: Substack lets independent writers and podcasters publish directly to their audience and get paid through subscriptions, https://substack.com

12. Patreon: https://www.patreon.com

13. Zillow: https://www.zillow.com

14. Compass: https://www.compass.com

15. Redfin: https://www.redfin.com

16. "A Comprehensive Guide to Digital Payments," https://www.entrust.com/resources/faq/guide-to-digital-payments

17. "New trends in US consumer digital payments," McKinsey & Company, https://www.mckinsey.com/industries/financial-services/our-insights/banking-matters/new-trends-in-us-consumer-digital-payments

18. Decentraland: Marketplace for collectables and art, https://market.decentraland. org

19. Matthew Ball, "The Metaverse: What It Is, Where to Find it, and Who Will Build It," January 2020 https://www.matthewball.vc/all/themetaverse

20. Metaverse: https://www.matthewball.vc/the-metaverse-primer

21. "Introducing Meta: A Social Technology Company," October 2021, https://about. fb.com/news/2021/10/facebook-company-is-now-meta

22. "NVIDIA Omniverse:The platform for creating and operating metaverse applications," https://www.nvidia.com/en-us/omniverse

23. "Microsoft to acquire Activision Blizzard to bring the joy and community of gaming to everyone, across every device," January 2022, https://news.microsoft. com/2022/01/18/microsoft-to-acquire-activision-blizzard-to-bring-the-joy-and-community-of-gaming-to-everyone-across-every-device/

24. "Gartner Predicts 25% of People Will Spend At Least One Hour Per Day in the Metaverse by 2026," February 2022, https://www.gartner.com/en/newsroom/press-releases/2022-02-07-gartner-predicts-25-percent-of-people-will-spend-at-least-one-hour-per-day-in-the-metaverse-by-2026

25. eBay: https://www.ebay.com

26. Amazon: https://www.amazon.com

27. Jeff Bezos, et al., "Method and system for placing a purchase order via a communications network," US Patent Application: US5960411, https:// worldwide.espacenet.com/publicationDetails/biblio?CC=US&NR=5960411&KC =&FT=E&locale=en_EP

28. Alex Cocotas, "How Priceline's Business Works," January 2012, https://www. businessinsider.com/how-pricelines-business-works

29. "Alibaba Business Model," The Business Model Analyst, April 2023, https:// businessmodelanalyst.com/alibaba-business-model/

30. TMall: Alibaba Cloud, https://www.alibabacloud.com/customers/tmall

31. TaskRabbit: Revolutionizing Everyday Work, https://www.taskrabbit.com/

32. "The Internet of Things: How to capture the value of IoT," McKinsey & Company, May 2018, https://www.mckinsey.com/~/media/McKinsey/ Business%20Functions/McKinsey%20Digital/Our%20Insights/The%20 Internet%20of%20Things%20How%20to%20capture%20the%20value%20of%20 IoT/How-to-capture-the-value-of-IoT.pdf

33. "Monetizing the Internet of Things: Extracting Value from the Connectivity Opportunity," Cap Gemini Consulting, 2014, iot_monetization_0.pdf, https://capgemini.com

34. Eden Estopace, "IDC forecasts connected IoT devices to generate 79.4ZB of data in 2025"

35. Petroc Taylor, "Big data market size revenue forecast worldwide from 2011 to 2027," July 2022, https://www.statista.com/statistics/254266/global-big-data-market-forecast/

36. Snowflake: https://www.snowflake.com/data-marketplace/

37. Amazon Data Exchange: https://aws.amazon.com/data-exchange/

38. Google: https://datasetsearch.research.google.com/

39. Red Hat: https://marketplace.redhat.com/en-us

40. Kaggle: https://www.kaggle.com/datasets

41. DATA.GOV: The Home of the U.S. Government's Open Data, https://www.data.gov/

42. Terbine: IoT Data Platform, https://terbine.com/

43. IOTA Foundation: https://data.iota.org/#/demo

44. i3 Systems Inc.: https://i3-iot.com/what-i3-does/

45. AWS IoT Core: https://aws.amazon.com/iot-core/?nc=sn&loc=2&dn=3

46. Karen Hao, "Tiny AI," MIT Technology Review, April 2020, https://www.technologyreview.com/technology/tiny-ai/

47. Pete Warden, "What's TinyML good for," Arm, https://www.youtube.com/watch?v=Wuq2aP5O5Z0

48. Harold Boley, "Expert system shells: very-high-level languages for Artificial Intelligence," Wiley Online Library, February 1990, https://onlinelibrary.wiley.com/doi/10.1111/j.1468-0394.1990.tb00158.x

49. "Expert Systems/Shells," https://en.wikibooks.org/wiki/Expert_Systems/Shells

50. Robert J. Mockler, "Developing Knowledge-Based Systems Using an Expert System Shell/Book and Disk Paperback," Peterson College Div., January 1992, https://www.amazon.com/Developing-Knowledge-Based-Systems-Expert-System/dp/0023818751

51. "IEEE Standard for Operator Interfaces of Artificial Intelligence," IEEE 2941.1-2022, March 2023, https://standards.icce.org/ieee/2941.1/10567/

52. Responsible AI Institute, https://www.responsible.ai/

53. Abhishek Kumar, et al., "Marketplace for AI Models," March 2020, Marketplace for AI Models, https://arXiv.org

54. "The State of AI in 2020: Global Survey," McKinsey, 2020, https://www.mckinsey.com/business-functions/mckinsey-analytics/our-insights/global-survey-the-state-of-ai-in-2020

55. "IDC Forecasts 18.6% Compound Annual Growth for the Artificial Intelligence Market in 2022-2026," July 2022, https://www.idc.com/getdoc.jsp?containerId=prEUR249536522

56. "AI Platform:Machine Learning on any data, of any size," Google, https://console.cloud.google.com/marketplace/details/google-cloud-platform/cloud-machine-learning-engine?pli=1

57. "Machine Learning Solutions," AWS Marketplace, https://aws.amazon.com/marketplace/solutions/machine-learning

58. Modzy: "Build Edge AI Solutions Faster," https://www.modzy.com/platform/ai-model-marketplace/

59. SeeMe.ai: "The no-code MLOps Platform," https://www.seeme.ai/

60. Bonseyes: An open platform for the development of systems of Artificial Intelligence from cloud to edge devices, https://www.bonseyes.eu/

61. Rishi Bommasani, et al., "On the Opportunities and Risks of Foundation Models," July 2022, https://arxiv.org/pdf/2108.07258.pdf

62. Aakanksha Chowdhery, et al., "PaLM: Scaling Language Modeling with Pathways," April 2022, https://storage.googleapis.com/pathways-language-model/PaLM-paper.pdf

63. Sharan Narang, et al., "Pathways Language Model (PaLM): Scaling to 540 billion Parameters for Breakthrough Performance," Blog, April 2022, https://ai.googleblog.com/2022/04/pathways-language-model-palm-scaling-to.html

64. Kush R. Varshney, "Trustworthy Machine Learning," February 2022, http://www.trustworthymachinelearning.com/

65. Regulation of Artificial Intelligence, Wikipedia, https://en.wikipedia.org/wiki/Regulation_of_artificial_intelligence

66. Andrew Smith, "Using Artificial Intelligence and Algorithms," April 2020, https://www.ftc.gov/business-guidance/blog/2020/04/using-artificial-intelligence-algorithms

67. "Liability for artificial intelligence and other emerging digital technologies," 2019, https://op.europa.eu/en/publication-detail/-/publication/1c5e30be-1197-11ea-8c1f-01aa75ed71a1/language-en

68. Eric Boyd, "Microsoft and Facebook create open ecosystem for AI model interoperability," September 2017, https://azure.microsoft.com/en-us/blog/microsoft-and-facebook-create-open-ecosystem-for-ai-model-interoperability/

69. "Adversarial Machine Learning," blog, IBM, 2018, https://researcher.watson.ibm.com/researcher/view_group.php?id=9571

70. Emma Strubell, et al., "Energy and Policy Considerations for Deep Learning in NLP," June 2019, https://arxiv.org/pdf/1906.02243.pdf

71. Tom Taulli, "API Economy: Is It the Next Big Thing?," January 2020, https://www.forbes.com/sites/tomtaulli/2020/01/18/api-economy--is-it-the-next-big-thing/#6f28b4c242ff

72. Celigo: Solving the Integration Challenge with iPaaS, https://www.celigo.com/

73. Plaid: APIs for financial transaction, https://plaid.com/

74. Zymr: Ecosystem connectors, https://www.zymr.com/ecosystem-connectors/

75. Rapid API: Ecosystem connectors, https://rapidapi.com/

76. Cloud Foundry: APIs, https://www.cloudfoundry.org/the-foundry/api-connect/

77. Rakuten: A place to share information for developers, https://developers.rakuten.com/

78. APILayer: Market API, https://promptapi.com/provider

79. Twilio: Platform for developers, https://www.twilio.com/

80. Yappes: API bazaar, https://yappes.com/

81. Akana: https://www.akana.com/products/api-platform

82. Akana: API Management Platform, https://www.akana.com/blog/api-economy

83. "Global API Management Market to be worth USD 6263 Million By 2028 with CAGR of 11.3% - Zion Market Research," September 2021, https://www.prnewswire.com/news-releases/global-api-management-market-to-be-worth-usd-6263-million-by-2028-with-cagr-of-11-3---zion-market-research-301377394.html

84. Wilson Mar, "API Development Ecosystem," 2023, https://wilsonmar.github.io/api-ecosystem/

85. "Top 10 Digital Twin Companies Impacting Industry 4.0 Innovations," April 2023, https://www.emergenresearch.com/blog/top-10-digital-twin-companies-impacting-industry-4-0-innovations-in-2021

86. "What is a digital twin?," IBM, https://www.ibm.com/topics/what-is-a-digital-twin

87. Enrique Andaluz, "The Process Digital Twin: A step toward operational excellence," October 2017, https://cloudblogs.microsoft.com/industry-blog/

manufacturing/2017/10/23/the-process-digital-twin-a-step-toward-operational-excellence/

88. Enrique Morales Orcajo, "6 Digital Twin Applications in Healthcare – The Revolution of the Next Decade," January 2021, https://www.linkedin.com/pulse/6-digital-twin-applications-healthcare-revolution-enrique/

89. Bosch IoT Suite, https://bosch-iot-suite.com/

90. Xometry: Manufacturing on Demand, https://www.xometry.com/

91. "Xometry Launches 2D Technical Drawing Marketplace," https://www.digitalengineering247.com/article/xometry-launches-2d-technical-drawing-marketplace/

92. Cad Crowd: Freelance CAD design, engineering, 3D modeling & drafting services, https://www.cadcrowd.com/

93. GrabCAD: Making Additive Manufacturing at Scale Possible, https://grabcad.com/

94. Kate Johnson, The Future of Media & Entertainment in the Experience Economy, https://cloudblogs.microsoft.com/industry-blog/microsoft-in-business/media-comm/2019/04/29/the-future-of-media-entertainment-in-the-experience-economy/

95. Jessica Bonacci, "80+ YouTube Marketing Statistics for 2023 That Will Blow Your Mind," https://www.webfx.com/blog/internet/youtube-marketing-statistics/

96. Barry Elad, "Media and Entertainment Industry Statistics and Facts," February 2023, https://www.enterpriseappstoday.com/stats/media-and-entertainment-industry-statistics.html

97. "Movies and Entertainment Market Size, Share & Trends Analysis," https://www.grandviewresearch.com/industry-analysis/movies-entertainment-market

98. Disney Plus: https://www.disneyplus.com/

99. NFL: https://www.nfl.com/videos/

100. Artlist: https://artlist.io/

101. "Power shifts: Altering the dynamics of the E&M industry," PWC Report, https://www.pwc.com/gx/en/entertainment-media/outlook-2021/perspectives-2021-2025.pdf

102. "Ecosystem 2.0: Climbing to the next level," McKinsey, September 2020, https://www.mckinsey.com/business-functions/mckinsey-digital/our-insights/ecosystem-2-point-0-climbing-to-the-next-level

103. "The gaming industry sees major revenue in going mobile," January 2022, https://www.marketplace.org/shows/marketplace-tech/the-gaming-industry-sees-major-revenue-in-going-mobile/

104. "Game on: An interview with Microsoft's head of gaming ecosystem," January 2022, https://www.mckinsey.com/industries/technology-media-and-telecommunications/our-insights/game-on-an-interview-with-microsofts-head-of-gaming-ecosystem

105. "Global Digital Games Market," EMR report, https://www.expertmarketresearch.com/reports/digital-games-market

106. ESPN: https://www.espn.com/

107. Josh Bersin, "Google for Jobs: Potential To Disrupt The $200 Billion Recruiting Industry," Forbes report, May 2017, https://www.forbes.com/sites/joshbersin/2017/05/26/google-for-jobs-potential-to-disrupt-the-200-billion-recruiting-industry/

108. ZipRecruiter: https://www.ziprecruiter.com/

109. Upwork: https://www.upwork.com/

110. Glassdoor: https://www.glassdoor.com

111. Monster: https://www.monster.com

112. TechRadar: https://www.techradar.com/reviews/monster

113. CareerBuilder: https://www.careerbuilder.com/

114. Facebook Marketplace: https://www.facebook.com/marketplace/learn-more/

115. Eventbrite: https://www.eventbrite.com/

116. Meetup: https://www.meetup.com/

117. OpenSports: https://opensports.net/

118. "Making Money with Stock Photography," https://shotkit.com/making-money-with-stock-photography/

119. Adobe Stock: https://stock.adobe.com/

120. Alamy: https://www.alamy.com

121. Shutterstock: https://www.shutterstock.com/about

122. Getty Images: https://www.gettyimages.com/

123. Getty Images: https://www.gettyimages.com/visual-gps/insights

124. Robyn Conti, "What Is An NFT? Non-Fungible Tokens Explained," March 2023, https://www.forbes.com/advisor/investing/cryptocurrency/nft-non-fungible-token/

125. Jack Caporal, "The NFT Market," February 2022, https://www.fool.com/the-ascent/research/nft-market/

126. OpenSea: https://opensea.io/

127. The Novatar: https://thenovatar.com/

128. NFT Marketplace: https://crypto.com/nft/marketplace

129. "Education Technology Market Size," GVR report, https://www. grandviewresearch.com/industry-analysis/education-technology-market

130. Byju's: Global edtech leader, https://byjus.com/us/

131. Anthology: Learners' portal, https://www.anthology.com

132. TPT: The go-to platform for supporting teachers, https://www. teacherspayteachers.com/

133. Udemy: Share the knowledge with the world, https://about.udemy.com/

134. Chegg: Strive to improve the overall return on investment in education, https://www.chegg.com/

135. Coursera: Learn without limits, https://www.coursera.org

136. EDX: https://www.edX.com/

137. Udacity: Turn talent into greatness, https://www.udacity.com/

138. Skillshare: Inspiring discovery through creativity, https://www.skillshare.com/

139. Randall Rothenberg, "Is Marketing a Strategic Resource or a Procured Commodity?," November 2009, https://www.iab.com/news/is-marketing-a-strategic-resource-or-a-procured-commodity/

140. Smaato: Solving Complexity with Simplicity, https://www.smaato.com/

141. InMobi Exchange: https://www.inmobi.com/exchange

142. IBM Developer: Learn in-demand skills, build solutions, https://developer.ibm.com/

143. Vimeo Livestream Production Services: https://livestream.com/production

144. iMovie: https://www.videowinsoft.com/imovie-movie-maker-mac.html

145. Walmart: https://www.walmart.com

146. Target: https://www.target.com

147. "Amazon marketplace statistics 2022," https://www.edesk.com/blog/amazon-statistics/

148. "How Many Sellers Are on Amazon?," 2023, https://www.helium10.com/blog/how-many-sellers-on-amazon/

149. "Amazon Personalize." https://aws.amazon.com/personalize/

150. "Pricing: The next frontier of value creation in private equity," McKinsey report, October 2019, https://www.mckinsey.com/business-functions/growth-marketing-and-sales/our-insights/pricing-the-next-frontier-of-value-creation-in-private-equity

151. Patrick Brüns, "The history of pricing: from the barter system to dynamic pricing," June 2020, https://aifora.com/en/blog-en/the-history-of-pricing-from-the-barter-system-to-dynamic-pricing/

152. Jennifer Dublino, "What Is Dynamic Pricing, and How Does It Affect E-commerce?," August 2023, https://www.business.com/articles/what-is-dynamic-pricing-and-how-does-it-affect-ecommerce/

153. Kelsey Coyle, et al., "2021 Findings from the Diary of Consumer Payment Choice," Federal Reserve Bank of San Francisco, May 2021, https://www.frbsf.org/cash/publications/fed-notes/2021/may/2021-findings-from-the-diary-of-consumer-payment-choice/

154. Alex Clere, "75% of consumers now using mobile wallets – survey," May 2022, https://fintechmagazine.com/digital-payments/75-of-consumers-now-using-mobile-wallets-survey

155. Richard Garlick, "Incentive Marketplace Estimate: Research Study," Incentive Federation Inc., 2022, https://www.incentivefederation.org/wp-content/uploads/2022/08/IFI-2022-Research-Study-Final-Report-1.pdf

156. "The value of getting personalization right—or wrong—is multiplying," McKinsey, November 2021, https://www.mckinsey.com/capabilities/growth-marketing-and-sales/our-insights/the-value-of-getting-personalization-right-or-wrong-is-multiplying

157. Anne Slough, "Conversational Interactions And AI: Enhancing the Digital Buying Experience and Closing Gaps In Your Sales Process," Forrester Report, July 2021, https://www.forrester.com/blogs/conversational-interactions-and-ai-enhancing-the-digital-buying-experience-and-closing-gaps-in-your-sales-process/

158. Kashmir Hill, "How Target Figured Out A Teen Girl Was Pregnant Before Her Father Did," Forbes, February 2012, https://www.forbes.com/sites/kashmirhill/2012/02/16/how-target-figured-out-a-teen-girl-was-pregnant-before-her-father-did/?sh=5647ceed6668

159. Google: Privacy Policy, https://policies.google.com/privacy?hl=en-US

160. IBM: Privacy Statement, July 2023, https://www.ibm.com/us-en/privacy

161. Microsoft: Privacy, https://privacy.microsoft.com/en-US/

162. "The critical role of reviews in Internet trust," https://cdn2.hubspot.net/hubfs/2749863/2019-trustpilot/The%20Critical%20Role%20of%20Reviews%20in%20Internet%20Trust%20(UK)%20-%20final.pdf

163. Georgios Askalidis and Edward C. Malthouse, "The value of online customer reviews," September 2016, https://www.scholars.northwestern.edu/en/publications/the-value-of-online-customer-reviews

164. "Customer Engagement, Made Simple with AI," Shopify AppStore, https://apps.shopify.com/

165. BigCommerce: Enterprise ecommerce, simplified, https://www.bigcommerce.com/

166. Peter Adams, "Amazon nears $10B in quarterly ad revenue while digital peers slump," October 2022, https://www.marketingdive.com/news/amazon-Q3-earnings-holiday-forecast-advertising/635227/

167. Yan Anderson, "How to Advertise in the Online Multi Vendor Marketplace," May 2021, https://www.cs-cart.com/blog/how-to-advertise-in-the-online-multi-vendor-marketplace/

168. Disney+ launches new ad tier — why it could be a $3 billion opportunity: Analyst," December 2022, https://finance.yahoo.com/news/disney-launches-new-ad-tier-why-it-could-be-a-3-billion-opportunity-analyst-202501704.html

169. "The (Ultimate) Guide for Marketplace Analytics," 2021, https://mixpanel.com/blog/ultimate-guide-marketplace-analytics/

170. "The ultimate marketplace analytics guide," https://e-tailize.com/blog/the-ultimate-marketplace-analytics-guide/

171. "What is a Membership Model," https://www.wildapricot.com/blog/membership-model#7-benefits-of-using-a-membership-model

172. Internal Revenue Service (IRS), US Federal Government, https://www.irs.gov/

173. Will Kenton, "Carrying Value: Definition, Formulas, and Example," October 2020, https://www.investopedia.com/terms/c/carryingvalue.asp

174. Brian Beers, "Examples of Barter Transactions," Investopedia, December 2022, https://www.investopedia.com/ask/answers/101314/what-are-some-examples-barter-transactions.asp

175. Corporation for Public Broadcasting, https://cpb.org/aboutcpb/

176. "Advertising revenue of Google from 2001 to 2022," https://www.statista.com/statistics/266249/advertising-revenue-of-google/

177. "Facebook Ad Revenue," https://www.oberlo.com/statistics/facebook-ad-revenue

178. Microsoft Financing Program Download: https://download.microsoft.com/download/3/9/0/390DF0B3-8B15-4E65-AF5E-71A7280E7682/Microsoft-Financing-Program-FAQ-Customer_en-US.pdf

179. IBM Financing: https://www.ibm.com/financing

180. "The leasing revenue model and leasing arrangements," https://learn.marsdd.com/article/the-leasing-revenue-model-and-leasing-arrangements/

181. "Real Estate Rental Global Market 2023," https://www.thebusinessresearchcompany.com/report/real-estate-rental-global-market-report

182. Analyze the effectiveness of spend-based commitments: https://cloud.google.com/billing/docs/how-to/cud-analysis-spend-based

183. "11 marketplace metrics you should be tracking to measure your success," September 2022, https://www.sharetribe.com/academy/measure-your-success-key-marketplace-metrics/

184. Gartner: Data Privacy Compliance, https://www.gartner.com/en/legal-compliance/insights/data-privacy-compliance

185. AI Fairness 360: Understand and mitigate bias in ML models, The Linux Foundation, https://ai-fairness-360.org/

186. AI Explainability 360: Understand how ML models predict labels, The Linux foundation, https://ai-explainability-360.org/

187. Adversarial Robustness Toolbox: A Python library for ML Security, The Linux Foundation, https://adversarial-robustness-toolbox.org/

188. Soumya Ghosh, et al., "Uncertainty Quantification 360: A Hands-on Tutorial," 2022, https://dl.acm.org/doi/fullHtml/10.1145/3493700.3493767

189. "Model interpretability," May 2023, https://learn.microsoft.com/en-us/azure/machine-learning/how-to-machine-learning-interpretability?view=azureml-api-2

190. "What Is Fairness and Model Explainability for Machine Learning Predictions?," https://docs.aws.amazon.com/sagemaker/latest/dg/clarify-fairness-and-explainability.html

191. "2020 United States federal government data breach," Wikipedia, https://en.wikipedia.org/wiki/2020_United_States_federal_government_data_breach

192. "Safeguarding artifact integrity across any software supply chain," https://slsa.dev/

193. The Software Package Data Exchange (SPDX), https://spdx.dev/

194. Runhua Xu, et al., "Privacy-Preserving Machine Learning: Methods, Challenges and Directions," September 2021, https://arxiv.org/abs/2108.04417

195. Vendavo: Pricing Software, https://www.vendavo.com/glossary/pricing-software/

196. SAP: https://www.sap.com

197. PROS: Develop Impactful Pricing Strategies with Cutting-Edge AI, https://pros.com/products/price-optimization-software/

198. Amazon Pricing Software: https://feedvisor.com/feedvisor-360/

199. Pricefx: Pricing Software and Optimization, https://www.pricefx.com/

200. Vistaar: Pricing Software, https://www.vistaar.com

201. EEXAR: Negotiation Software, https://www.eexar.com/eexar-negotiation/

202. Zoho Contracts: Contract Negotiation, https://www.zoho.com/contracts/negotiation.html

203. DocSend: A tool for better sales negotiation, not enablement, https://www.docsend.com/blog/improve-sales-negotiation-with-docsend/

204. "A Guide to Marketplaces: Third Edition," https://versionone.vc/marketplaces-guide-ed3/

205. "Cross-Border B2C E-Commerce Market Share," Polaris Market Research, https://www.polarismarketresearch.com/industry-analysis/cross-border-b2c-e-commerce-market

206. "Cross-Border eCommerce – State Of The Art," https://gepard.io/ecommerce-strategy/cross-border-ecommerce

207. Lyft: https://www.lyft.com

208. Adobe: https://www.adobe.com/

209. TikTok: https://www.tiktok.com/en/

210. Marketoonist: a content marketing studio, www.marketoonist.com

211. "VAT on e-Commerce," https://vat-one-stop-shop.ec.europa.eu/index_en

212. FTC: "International Consumer Protection and Cooperation," https://www.ftc.gov/policy/international/international-consumer-protection-cooperation